Bridge for Beginners

Bridge for Beginners

A Step-by-Step Guide to
One of the Most Challenging Card Games

Paul Mendelson

The Lyons Press
Guilford, Connecticut
An imprint of The Globe Pequot Press

Dedication

To Gareth and Katy
—perfect candidates for this book.

To buy books in quantity for corporate use
or incentives, call **(800) 962–0973**
or e-mail **premiums@GlobePequot.com**.

The Lyons Press is an imprint of The Globe Pequot Press.

10   9   8   7   6   5

Printed in the United States of America

Designed by Maggie Peterson

ISBN 978-1-59228-283-8

Library of Congress Cataloging-in-Publication Data is
available on file.

Contents

Part Three

Part Four

Glossary

Index

Introduction

Bridge is the ultimate game. It is truly a mind-sport, for it is as taxing on the brain as a decathlon is on the body. The beauty of bridge is that whatever your standard you will always gain pleasure from it. It is hugely social, always leads to an expanding circle of friends and, on more than one occasion, has led to marriage—but don't let that put you off! It is absorbing, all-consuming and, I have to confess, pretty addictive.

Anything worth learning is going to take effort; bridge is no exception. The first few weeks of lessons (or sections of this book) will tax you and you will need time to practice, read, and re-read. Ideally, you will have friends or relatives who play who can advise you, or adult education or bridge club classes you can attend locally. However, when the going gets tough, just remember your friends who play, think of the most foolish you know, and tell yourself that if he or she can master it, then so will you.

Actually, you will never master bridge. No one has yet. Bob Hamman, the world champion since 1985, famously said, "The world's best players aren't very good, and everyone else is a whole lot worse…" That is the great challenge that bridge poses.

In *Bridge for Complete Beginners* no knowledge of the game is assumed. Right from the beginning, you will be led through the key basic principles to ensure that you have a solid grounding on which to build. With these basics established, you will be ready to go as far as you want, whether your aspirations are merely social bridge, club bridge, competitive bridge, or trialing for the national team. My aspiration for you, right now, is to make you a popular, winning, social bridge player—a player all your friends will want to have at their bridge afternoons and/or evenings.

The advantage of this book is that you won't miss classes, get ahead or behind anyone else: you have the material at your fingertips and you can move at the pace that you set yourself.

Bridge is divided into two parts: the bidding (or auction) and the play of the cards. Each is examined here. The play is pretty much universal; the language of the bidding varies from country to country. However, once you have a grasp of the basic Acol system that is played throughout the world, you will be able to adapt quite quickly to versions, or dialects, of this bridge language in other parts of the world.

It is enormous fun to play bridge in foreign countries. You get to meet so many new people, with an instant interest in common. Bridge is a global phenomenon. Great players have emerged from both North and South America, the UK and the rest of Europe—perhaps most notably Italy—and, now, the Pacific Rim countries. China has become obsessed by the game and it will not be long before they challenge for the world championship. Gone too are the days when bridge was merely for the older generation. Many children are offered the chance to learn the game at school and university, and continue playing all their lives. Of course, many older people still play and will continue to do so; I have students aged thirteen to ninety-three. Trials in America have found that bridge is particularly effective at stimulating and exercising the brain, fighting the onset of mental degeneration. So it's official: bridge is good for you.

As a mental challenge, it is unsurpassed. As a social experience, it is fantastic. As a gymnasium for the brain, it is the ultimate workout.

Enjoy.

PART ONE

Introduction to Bridge: How It Is Played and Scored

1

Absolute Beginners

Bridge is a game for four people. Throughout the ages, the world over, bridge players have been heard wailing because they can find three players but not a fourth. Thankfully, when learning, you can be on your own, with a mate, or have a complete four. If you're learning on your own, simply pretend that you're playing with three others and play their cards as well as your own.

Dealing the Cards

Before we learn anything further about the game, let's get some cards in your hands. Use a full deck of fifty-two cards, removing the jokers, which are not needed for bridge. Give the pack a good shuffle and then start dealing the cards to the four people around the table. Thankfully, dealing is easy. You start with the player on your left and then deal one card to each player facedown in a clockwise direction until you run out of cards. If you've dealt correctly, from a full pack, you will deal everyone thirteen cards each and yourself the final card.

Sorting Your Hand

Once the deal is complete, everyone picks up their cards without showing them to anyone else, and sorts them into groups of cards of the same suit: all the spades together, hearts, diamonds, and clubs. Because it's easy to mistake cards in the heat of play, I recommend sorting them so that the suits run black-red-black-red. In this way, even after a glass or two of that excellent Chardonnay of yours, you'll still be able to pull out the right card. If you can, try to arrange your cards in a fan, facing you and out of view of the other players at your table. If this seems difficult at first, you'll get used to it once you play cards for a few days.

Evaluating Your Hand

Now, look at your cards. Have you got a good hand or a bad hand? How do you know? There are several ways to evaluate a hand of cards at bridge, but the most important is by counting your points. Points, for hand evaluation, are allocated to aces and picture cards only. These are calculated as follows:

ace	=	4 points
king	=	3 points
queen	=	2 points
jack	=	1 point

So, if your hand looks like this, how many points is it worth?

♠ KJ74
♥ A9632
♦ Q73
♣ 4

You have four points in the spade suit, four in the heart suit, two in the diamond suit, and none in the club suit. So, your hand is worth ten points. This would be an average hand in bridge because there are four suits and each is headed by the ace-king-queen-jack, and each of those holdings is worth ten points.

♠ AKQJ =		10 points
♥ AKQJ =		10 points
♦ AKQJ =		10 points
♣ AKQJ =		10 points

So, the total number of points in a pack of cards is forty. On average, each player will receive one quarter of those points—ten. The interesting thing is that this almost never happens and sometimes you are dealt a huge number of points; other times just a few.

If the hand at which you are looking contains more than ten points then you have a better than average hand; if your hand contains fewer than ten points, you have a worse than average hand. Check with your friends—or by looking at the hands—that the total number of points at your table equals forty.

The Order of the Suits
You may have noticed that when a bridge hand is displayed—here in this book, or in newspapers, books, or

magazines the world over—the layout is always the same. Spades at the top, hearts next, then diamonds, and finally clubs. This is because, in bridge, the suits have a pecking order and it is always like this:

- ♠ spades
- ♥ hearts
- ♦ diamonds
- ♣ clubs

This is of significance throughout the game of bridge and you will find that, soon, you cannot imagine ever having thought of cards in any other way.

There are other factors involved in assessing the strengths and weaknesses of the bridge hand you are holding but, for the moment, the point total is the simplest and the best. As you move on, we will add other elements into the equation. So, now that you know whether your hand is better or worse than average, what next? Well, to give you some idea of what the game is about, it is time to play a hand of bridge. If you are on your own, you can turn up the other hands you have dealt and sort them into suits; if you have friends with you, keep your cards hidden. As an exercise, we are going to play the hand.

To start with, I want you, as the player who dealt the cards, to "lead" one by placing a card face up in the middle of the table. In bridge, which card you play is vital but, for the moment, play any card you like—high or low. Everything moves clockwise in bridge. The player to your left must then play a card of the same suit, then the next player and finally the fourth player. Whoever has played the highest card gathers together all four cards, places them facedown in a neat little pile in front of him or her and is said to have won "the trick."

Tricks

A trick is four cards—one from each player—and is won by the player who played the highest card. In bridge the ace is the highest card; the 2 is the lowest.

The person who won that trick then leads the first card to the next trick. It can be the same suit, or a different one. For now, it doesn't matter. Try leading a high card, and you will see that everyone else probably plays their lowest card in the suit; try playing a low one and then each player may try to win the trick with increasingly high cards. All we are doing for the moment is getting used to the play of the cards and watching what happens. Continue playing like this until all your cards are gone. If you cannot play a card in the suit that is led, you will have to play a little card in another suit. This is called discarding.

At the end of the hand, when all the cards have been played, there should be thirteen tricks shared between the four players. If there are not, something has gone wrong (maybe there are cards left in the box!). You will notice, usually, that the hand that had the most points will win the most tricks. So, we can begin to understand that, basically, the more points you have, the more tricks you can expect to make. But there are two other vital factors:

1. If you are on lead, you have a big advantage because if you play a card in a suit in which no other player has any cards left, you will automatically win that trick.

2. If you hold length in a suit (that is to say five cards or more), then this is a great feature. Imagine for a

moment that you held this hand (it's never likely to happen in real life, but it demonstrates this principle well)…

♠ AKQJ1098765432

♥ –

♦ –

♣ –

…and you were first to play. You would probably play A♠— no one else would have any spades, so you would win the trick and still be on lead. You would play K♠ and, again, you would win. You would continue winning every trick because no one else had spades to play. Eventually the other players at your table would have to throw away aces and kings in the other suits on your spades, and you would end up with all thirteen tricks. Notice that you only held ten points, but you made all the tricks. This is because holding a long suit is a huge asset in bridge.

Now, gather together all the cards, give them a good shuffle and then let the player to your left deal them out again, starting with the player to his or her left until they have all been played (remember that the last card should go to the dealer—if not, there has been a misdeal).

Sort the cards into suits again and add up your points, referring if necessary to the chart on page 4.

Bridge Is a Partnership Game

We are going to play out the hand again, but this time we must introduce a vital element of bridge. It is a game played in partnerships. Look up at the player sitting opposite you (if you are by yourself, imagine that it is avid bridge players Bill Gates and tennis great Martina Navratilova) and smile warmly at him or her (we'll assume your partner is male from now on, just to simplify things). You will have to work as a partnership to succeed at bridge, so you might as well make him feel that you are pleased to be his partner and, hopefully, he will do the same.

When it comes to the play of the cards, the significance of playing as partners is this: if your partner is winning the trick for your side, you don't need to win it again. Let me show you what I mean.

In the following diagram, you will see that there is a small box, denoting the bridge table, with the compass points shown. This is the standard way of illustrating players' positions at the table. The partnerships are therefore North-South playing against East-West. You will often see these abbreviated to N/S and E/W.

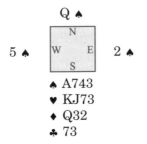

It is the first trick of the hand. You are South. Your opponent, West, has played 5♠, your partner, North, has played Q♠ and East who, presumably, cannot beat the queen, has just played a low spade. You too should play your lowest spade—3♠—because your partner has already won the trick for your side with his queen.

The player who wins a trick plays the first card to the next trick—in this case, North.

Traditionally, the partner of the player who wins the first trick for his side collects up the trick, and all subsequent tricks taken by his side, and arranges them in front of him neatly. There will be, therefore, only two players collecting the tricks won—one player from each side.

Try playing out all thirteen tricks now, remembering that you are playing as a partnership. Before playing, note how many points you have between you as a partnership—write it down if necessary—and then see how many tricks each partnership wins. You will find—usually—that the side that has the most points will win the majority of the tricks. If they do not, it may be because you played badly (what else can you do when you have only ten minutes of experience?) or because one player had a very long suit and was able to take lots of tricks because no else held any more cards in that suit. In bridge, we are only interested in taking the majority of the tricks, so if you made five or six tricks, that's fine, but it's not really important in bridge terms, as you'll see shortly.

Once you have completed this hand, gather up the cards once again, give them a good shuffle, and then, continuing to move in a clockwise direction, let the next player deal out the cards. This time, we will introduce a new element into the play of the cards—"trumps."

Trumps

A trump suit is a suit that for the duration of the hand becomes the most important suit in the pack. How you choose which suit this will be is part of the game of bridge and we'll talk about it a bit later on. So far, in the hands you have played, you have played them in no-trumps—that is to say, without a master suit. This happens quite a bit in bridge, but more often than not there is a trump suit.

Arrange your cards, add up your points and, talking across the table to your partner, discuss how many points you have as a partnership. You wouldn't be able to do this if you were playing for real. You would have to use the special bridge language or code to discuss this, but that will come later. Check that the combined point-count of the two partnerships adds up to forty. If it doesn't, have another go, checking the point valuations in the chart on page 4.

For now, we will let the partnership with the most points between them choose which suit they want to have as the master suit—the trump suit. For this exercise, you can show one another your cards. Look for a suit in which you and your partner hold at least eight cards between your two hands. Eight is an important number because it means that your side holds the clear majority of cards in that suit. Seven trumps between you are adequate but it still leaves six trumps for your opponents, so we much prefer to look for eight trumps. After all, if you are going to have a master suit, you might as well pick one where you have plenty more than the opposition. It doesn't matter whether you have high cards in the suit or only low ones; the important bit is quantity—that you have at least eight of them between your two hands.

If you find that you have no suit with at least eight cards between you, then normally you would opt to play this hand in no-trumps—without a trump suit—but, for the purposes of this exercise, steal a little card from one of your opponents' hands so that you have eight cards in one suit between your hand and your partner's hand. Remember to give your generous opponent a card back in another suit or you will have fourteen cards and he will only have twelve and that, I can tell you, will not be a success.

Whichever suit you choose will be the master suit for the duration of this hand. Let's say, for example, that it is spades. Now we will witness the value of a trump suit. As before, the player who dealt the cards leads the first card—it can be a card from the trump suit if you like, or something else. For now, it doesn't matter.

The Value of Trumps

Continue playing out the cards as before, remembering that you are playing as a partnership. However, if you—or your opponents—run out of the suit that has been led but you have cards in the trump suit, you can play one of these cards—the lowest will do—and, because it is the master suit, that will win the trick. Look at this example that occurs mid-way through a hand. You are South again:

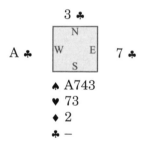

3 ♣

A ♣   N / W / E / S   7 ♣

♠ A743
♥ 73
♦ 2
♣ —

Quite a few tricks have been played. Then your opponent, West, leads A♣. Your partner plays a little one, as does your right-hand opponent. Because you have no clubs left in your hand, usually you would lose the trick, but because you have spades as the trump suit and you cannot follow suit, you can play a spade and this will win the trick—beating even an ace in another suit. So, you play 3♠—there is no need to play a higher one—and you can claim the trick because you "trumped." The old-fashioned term "to ruff" or "ruffed" means the same thing and is often used. You gather up the trick and lead to the next one.

Note that you can only trump if you have no cards in the suit that has been led. If you do have cards in the suit that has been led, you must play one: it is illegal—within the rules of the game, that is—not to do so (see Basic Rules on page 162).

Also, towards the end of the game, it may be that both you and another opponent have no cards in the suit led. If you trump in with a low card, your opponent may trump in with a higher card in the trump suit. That is known as an overruff—or being overtrumped.

For this reason, sometimes the players who have chosen the trump suit will opt to play out the high cards in the trump suit early on in order to pull out the remaining cards in the trump suit from the opponents' hands. This is known as "drawing trumps."

When, why, and how we do this will be discussed later.

The value of a trump suit varies enormously from hand to hand and, of course, is hugely affected by how you play the cards. Hopefully, as you play this and other practice hands, you will see that there is a great advantage to being the side to choose which suit will be trumps.

The Contract

The next element of the puzzle is that of the "contract" at bridge. When you play, you and your partner do not simply try to make as many tricks as possible. Instead, one partnership will end up announcing that they will make a certain number of the thirteen tricks and then they must make that number. Failing to make that number of tricks carries twin penalties. First, your side of the scorecard will remain empty. Second, your opponents will receive a penalty score since you failed to fulfill your contract. Making more tricks than you say you will is OK, but the skill of the game lies in trying to estimate accurately how many of the thirteen tricks you will make and then making them. As mentioned earlier, we are not interested in making the minority of the tricks. The least number that concerns us is seven tricks—the slight majority—right up to and including all thirteen tricks.

To Summarize

Let's see now whether we can begin to paint a picture about how the game of bridge works:

Bridge is divided into two parts. The first element is the bidding or auction, during which you and your partner—and sometimes your opponents as well—describe to one another (using bridge language only) what you have in your hand in order to establish two main facts:

1. How many points you and your partner hold between you—the more points you hold, the more tricks you are likely to make. If your side holds the majority of points then, usually, your side will make the majority of tricks.

2. What your hand looks like in terms of the distribution of cards. Here you are seeking at least eight cards in the same suit between your two hands to name as your master suit. Failing that, you may opt to play the hand in "no-trumps" where there is no trump or master suit.

The second part of the game is the play of the cards. Here, you and your partner attempt to make the number of tricks you say you will and your opponents try to stop you from doing so. Whatever happens here will determine who scores what on the scorecard.

How these mechanisms work and how the game is scored will be dealt with in the ensuing pages. Already, you may find that the game is quite difficult to grasp, but the good news is this: the pieces will come together and soon you will have a clear idea of the game—and what a fascinating challenge it presents. Also, everything you learn now will be useful to you for the rest of your bridge-playing life. There is almost nothing of which you learn now that you have to unlearn later on. Since all these elements are repeated for every hand of bridge you play, you do not need to remember anything. Hopefully you have a grasp of the basic outline of the game now, and you are ready to start filling in the quite substantial gaps.

In the next section, we will look at how we estimate how many tricks we are going to make and then we will see the first elements of this strange bridge language we must master. But, before all that, there is one final basic of the game to which you need to be introduced—the concept of "the dummy."

The Dummy

When bridge was being played at the beginning of the twentieth century it was the preserve of the wealthy. Four chaps were playing in a gentlemen's club and the service was slow…They started complaining and eventually, unable to wait for their drinks any longer, the partner of the person with the strongest hand, who had declared that his side would make a certain number of tricks, got up from the table, threw down his cards faceup, and announced that his partner would play his hand as well as his own. It was a momentous occasion. From then on, every deal features one "dummy" hand opposite the player who first names the suit that becomes trumps. Exactly when, why, and who will all be explained in the following pages, but now we know that when you play the hand, you will be alone, playing your partner's cards as well as your own and everyone at the table will be able to see half the deck: thirteen cards in their own hand and thirteen laid out on the table. You would think it easy to be able to work out which of the two remaining people held which cards—if only it were...

2

The Game Unveiled

We're going to continue with our practice hands introducing new features, including the dummy, as we go. For the moment, we are going to chat in English across the table instead of the bridge language we would use in a real game of bridge.

Deal the cards again and sort them into suits and count your points. Once you have done this, chat with your partne

inform

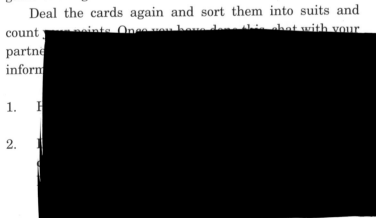

1.

2.

Although the side with the minority of points can cause difficulties for their opponents, usually it is the partnership with the majority of points that gets to decide which suit will be trumps. So, here, whichever side holds the majority of the points can choose which suit they want as trumps or, if they hold no suit with at least eight cards between their two hands, they can opt to play in no-trumps.

If you have dealt a hand where the points are divided 20–20 between the two partnerships then, for the purposes of this practice, it will be better to re-deal the hand.

So the partnership with the majority of points decides in which trump denomination, or suit, their side will play, but they must also contract themselves to make a certain number of tricks. The following chart gives you an idea of how many tricks you should expect to make depending upon how many points you hold as a partnership. Bear in mind that when there is a trump suit this chart is only a very rough guide—distribution and play will make a huge difference. For no-trump contracts, which rely almost entirely on the strength of the high cards, it is much more accurate.

Remember that we are not interested in making the minority of the tricks, so only contracts promising to make seven tricks or more are important.

You will notice that there are some overlaps in the point-counts. This is because, as you will see, points are not the only factors that determine the strength of our hand. Depending upon the distribution of our hand, you sometimes need fewer or more points to make certain contracts.

The final "level" column refers to the way we view bridge contracts at bridge and also the auction or bidding element of the game. Because only the majority of the tricks interest us, the first six tricks are taken for granted. So, if we are trying to make seven tricks, the contract is said to be at the 1-level, because it is one trick over the first six, and so on.

This will become clearer in the pages to follow.

So, let's imagine what might be happening at your table, and look at this hand as an example:

partner
♠ KQ75
♥ Q3
♦ K643
♣ 964

```
      N
  W       E
      S
```

you
♠ A8432
♥ AK85
♦ Q2
♣ 73

You and your partner add up your points and find that your side holds the majority. You—the South hand—hold 13pts. Your partner—North—holds 10pts. That gives you 23pts between you, and leaves your opponents with only 17pts (that gives us a combined total of 40pts, which is the full deck).

So, for this illustration, N/S will discuss with one another which suit should be trumps. Once you start playing for real, you will use bridge language but, for the moment, let's see what the players would say in English: North and South will tell each other (and their opponents who will be listening) in which suits they hold length. They will not bother to mention suits that do not contain at least four cards in them (half of the eight you are seeking), however good the cards may be. In bridge, you never mention three-card suits or two-card suits, even if they are all aces and kings.

South might tell his partner that he holds length in spades. North would be happy to have spades as trumps. Since South is suggesting them as trumps, he must have at least four of them—North holds four, so he knows that, as a partnership, they hold at least eight spades between them. North and South will then decide together how many tricks their side can make. Usually one player can work out the points held by his partner and then make a decision. Here, North will do this by finding out how many points his partner has and adding those to his. He can then consult the chart on page 18 to remind himself of how many tricks he is likely to make and then bid as many as he thinks his side can make. With 23pts between North and South, the expectation would be to make eight tricks, i.e. to play at the 2-level (two tricks over the first six which are taken for granted).

The Declarer

Now let's see how the game would get under way. South—the player who first mentioned the suit that is trumps—is going to play the hand (i.e. he plays both his own cards and those of his partner, the dummy). He is called "the de-clarer" because he is the member of the partnership who first mentioned spades—the suit that has been agreed by the partnership as trumps for this deal. The contract here is, technically speaking, "2 Spades" because South is going to try to make eight tricks (six plus two) with spades as the trump suit.

The player on the declarer's left (West) leads the first card and once he has placed his card down on the table the dummy will appear. North lays his cards down in neat rows on the table in front of him, with the trump suit put down first on the declarer's left, followed by the other suits in alternate colors.

When it is the turn of the dummy to play, the declarer leans over the table, selects which card he wants to play and places it on the trick. The next opponent plays and then the declarer will play a card from his own hand. Obviously, if the dummy is winning the trick already, declarer does not need to win the trick again for his side, and he plays low from his hand. If declarer wins a trick in the dummy hand, then he leads first from the dummy hand to the next trick. If he wins the trick in his own hand, the rule is that he leads from his own hand.

Notice that everyone at the table can see half the deck—their own hand and dummy—but the declarer has the slight advantage because he can see his partner's hand opposite him.

What does the dummy do now? Nothing. He remains quiet and does not become involved in the hand unless there is a problem with the rules. This is very rare and, for this reason, many dummies get up, stroll around, have a drink or just stretch their legs while their partner is playing the hand. Whatever happens, don't get into the habit of telling your partner what to do when you are dummy. It is not allowed and it is very distracting to your partner.

Finally, when all the cards have been played, you count up how many tricks your side made. If South made eight tricks or more, then he fulfilled this contract and he will be rewarded on the scorecard. If he fails to make his eight tricks—even if it is only by one trick—then he has failed to fulfill the contract and his opponents will gain a penalty score on the scorecard.

Once again, there is a lot here; the basic ideas behind the game, the concept of the dummy, and all the ritual of who leads when and how. Do not try to remember it all. It will occur every time you play the game and it will soon sink in.

3

The Scoring

Before beginning to learn the language of bridge, it is important to look at our targets—why we bother to go to all this trouble.

If we sit down to play bridge, we embark upon "a rubber" of bridge. A rubber is the best of three games. Whichever side wins two games—whether it is 2–0 or 2–1—wins the rubber. Think of it like a three-set tennis match where the winner is the player who wins two sets.

In order to score the important points at bridge, you have to bid and make contracts. Defeating your opponents wins you points, but they are not vital ones. Making extra tricks over and above your contract (known as "overtricks"), also scores you these second-class points. To score the important ones, you have to bid and make your contracts.

A bridge scorecard looks something like this:

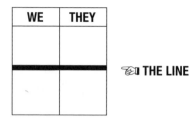

WE	THEY

☞ THE LINE

You will hear players talking about "the line" on a scorecard. The line is the thick horizontal line across the middle of the scorecard. Every contract you successfully make gets scored below the line; everything else gets scored above the line.

In order to win a game, and subsequently the rubber, you must score 100pts or more below the line. These points have nothing to do with the hand-evaluation points we looked at earlier—these are the scoring points. So, how do we score them? Let's look at the order of suits again:

	NT no-trumps	40pts for the first trick; 30pts per trick afterwards
major suits	♠ spades	30pts per trick
	♥ hearts	30pts per trick
minor suits	♦ diamonds	20pts per trick
	♣ clubs	20pts per trick

At the top of the list is no-trumps—the most important denomination and also the highest scoring. Spades and hearts are called the "major suits" because they score quite well—30pts per trick. Finally, there are diamonds and clubs. These are the "minor suits" because they are at the bottom of the order of priority and also the lowest scoring—just 20pts per trick.

Let's see how this works. Let us imagine that you and your partner decided that you could make eight tricks with spades as trumps. That would be a contract of 2 Spades—meaning the first six tricks, plus the two further tricks you have promised to try to make—with spades as trumps. You then play out the cards and you find that you do indeed make eight tricks. How do you score this? The contract was 2 Spades, so you score 2 x 30pts = 60pts. Because you bid and made your contract, these points go below the line…everything you B-b-b-bid goes B-b-b-below the line.

So, the scorecard now looks like this:

WE	THEY
60	

The 60pts get scored below the line in the "We" column. Anything your opponents score, you will mark down in the "They" column. You have now made what we call a "part-score." You have got part of the way towards your 100pts or more below the line. The next contract that you make will only need to score you 40pts in order to bring your total to 100pts and for you to score (win) the first game.

On the next hand, you bid 2 Hearts (2H) and you make eight tricks. That scores you another 60pts and will give you game. This is what your scorecard should look like now:

WE	THEY
60	
60	

Draw a line under your score, right across both columns, to indicate that this is game. You are now leading 1–0 and you must score only one more game to win the rubber. When you do that, you will receive a big bonus.

If you fail to make your contract or if you make over-tricks—tricks over and above what you said you would make—these get scored above the line. They do not count towards game but will be added up at the end of the rubber. For full details of scoring look at chapter 19, Scoring, on page 153.

Let's just complete our practice scoring session with the next contract. This time, you and your partner have lots of points between you and also plenty of spades. You think you will make ten tricks with spades as trumps—a contract of 4 Spades. You actually make eleven tricks. So, below the line, you score what you bid: 4 x 30pts = 120pts. Above the line you score 30pts, because you made one trick in spades over what you said you would. As you will see later, you receive a big bonus of 700pts for winning the rubber 2–0 and you are the champs. Filled in with these scores, your scorecard should look like this:

WE	THEY
700	
30	
60	
60	
120	

Under the new line you drew, you have now scored the 120pts for a contract of 4 Spades made, and a further 30pts above the line for the overtrick.

Finally, you add a bonus of 700pts above the line because, now that you have won two games, you have also won the rubber—without your opponents scoring anything. For winning the rubber by two games to nothing, you receive a 700pts bonus (you would receive a 500pts bonus by winning two games to one). Your total points score in the rubber was 970pts to nothing. See page 153 for full scoring details.

When the rubber is over, you can choose to play another against the same opponents, perhaps change partners or, if you are playing in a club, switch tables with other pairs. A rubber of bridge may last ten minutes or two hours and bridge players have been known to play for anything from fifteen minutes to twenty-four hours without stopping.

Game Contracts and Part-Scores

Notice how you can score game either by making several little contracts—known as part-scores—or by saying that you will make lots of tricks and scoring enough to give you game all in one hand. These contracts are known as "game contracts." And it is here that we see the real significance of the scoring system and the order of the suits. If you wanted to score 100pts below the line all in one go—a game contract—with clubs or diamonds as trumps, you would need to make eleven tricks: 5 Clubs (5C) or 5 Diamonds (5D) in order to score game (5 x 20pts = 100pts).

However, if you wanted to try to score game in one go with spades or hearts as trumps, because they score 30pts per trick you only need to make ten tricks: 4 Hearts (4H) or 4 Spades (4S) in order to score game (4 x 30pts = 120pts). Unfortunately, three tricks of 30pts only makes 90pts and are not enough to score game all in one go.

Now, think about no-trumps—that strange system whereby you score 40pts for the first trick in no-trumps and 30pts for all the rest. Why is that? Well 40 + 30 + 30 = 100, so if you want to try to make a game contract all in one go without a trump suit, in no-trumps, then you only need to make nine tricks—3NT.

Slams

What happens if you have been dealt masses of high card points between you and your partner and you think you might make twelve tricks or even all thirteen. This doesn't happen very often, but when it does it is worth bidding these contracts known as "slams." Saying you will make twelve tricks (a 6-level contract) is a "Small Slam"; trying to make all thirteen tricks (a 7-level contract) is a "Grand Slam." If you succeed, there are very worthwhile bonuses that get scored above the line, as well as making a game contract below the line.

But these are matters for the more experienced player. So far, we have no idea how to make ourselves understood in bridge language, so that is our next task. Here, at least, we have seen why we bother with the bidding and the play: our target on each hand is to try—if we have been dealt good enough cards—to make a part-score or a game contract. Once we have two games on the scorecard, we will win the rubber and receive the big bonus at the end for winning this particular match.

4

The Shape of the Hand

As well as point-count, there is one other crucial factor we must address when describing what we have in our hand to our partner: shape.

The good news is that there are only two shapes of hand you can have: **a balanced hand** where you have roughly the same number of cards in each suit, and an unbalanced hand, called **a distributional hand,** where you have one or two suits that are much longer than the others.

There is a simple test to carry out on your hand to ascertain whether it is balanced or distributional: Your hand is balanced if you have no more than eight cards in your two longest suits; it is distributional if you hold nine cards or more in your two longest suits.

So, let's see some examples:

a)   ♠ A74   b)   ♠ KQ754   c)   ♠ 8
        ♥ AK85   ♥ AQ73   ♥ AJ8643
        ♦ Q62   ♦ K6   ♦ KJ753
        ♣ J73   ♣ 96   ♣ 9

a) Balanced: as flat as a pancake. No more than seven cards between the longest suits. This hand could not be more balanced. 4–3–3–3 shape means every suit has almost the same number of cards.

b) Distributional. The hand contains nine cards between its two longest suits: spades and hearts, with two doubletons (suits with only two cards in them) as the outside suits.

c) Distributional. In fact, very distributional. A 6–5 distribution is uncommon. When you describe your hand to your partner in bridge language, you would emphasize that you hold great length in these two suits—hearts and diamonds—and you would want to ensure that one of them is chosen as your trump suit.

The Importance of Shape

What is the significance of a balanced and a distributional hand? Well, it is your first idea as to what might happen on the hand. If your hand is balanced, then you would suggest a no-trump contract to your partner because you have no one suit which dominates your hand and suggests itself as a trump suit (your partner may though—and he will tell you about that later on).

With a distributional hand, your first thought will be to have one of your long suits as the trump suit—if your partner's hand contains some support for you (cards in your suit).

You may end up in no-trumps, or even in one of your partner's suits as trumps, but you will have described your hand accurately and been able to make an informed decision.

So, during your conversation with your partner, you will attempt to impart how many points your hand contains. Then, with reference to the chart on page 18, you can work out how many tricks you are likely to take, and then which suit or suits are longest in your hand (remember, the number of cards held in a suit is more important than the strength of the cards held). You are looking to find a fit with partner's hand (eight cards or more between the two hands in the same suit) or you may decide that a contract without trumps (NTs) is a better idea.

The Dreaded 4–4–4–1 Hand

Let's have a quick word about hands with three 4-card suits and a singleton—the so-called 4–4–4–1 hands. These seem balanced (no more than eight cards between your two longest suits), but in fact they are not, because they also contain a singleton. This shape of hand is a real problem because it is neither balanced, nor is it really a distributional hand. Your best bet when opening the bidding with a 4–4–4–1 hand—and bridge has a lot to do with assessing the best choice out of a set of bad alternatives—is to say "No-bid" even with 12 or 13pts, but with 14pts to open the bidding with one of your suits and, if partner bids the suit in which you hold a singleton, rebid no-trumps at your next chance. It's not a perfect solution, but it works pretty well.

5

The Bidding
(AKA The Auction)

This is a major hurdle for you to overcome. The good news is that once you've got it, you or your opponents or all of you will be doing this on every hand of bridge you play. Within a month, you won't even be thinking about it.

The Price of Information

When bridge was first played, the bidding was a much more haphazard affair—not the detailed description we give these days—and it was run in the form of an auction. The auction element has been retained and it is the side promising to make the most tricks that gets to choose the trump suit—a huge advantage, you will remember. But that's not all—I feel a bit like an "infomercial" here—there's more!

Every time you describe your hand to your partner, you will be promising to make tricks, and the more information you impart, the higher the number of tricks will rise. So you have to be accurate and economical and the language that was invented for bridge makes that very difficult.

Before you wonder why you are doing this, reflect on all the other famous games we have invented. Golf would be easy if the holes weren't so small, and there were no bunkers, rough, or water; tennis is a fun game, I love it, but that damn net keeps getting in the way. All games have their built-in restrictions to make life harder for the players and, with bridge, it's just the same.

You will remember from chapter 1 that you are not interested in making the minority of the tricks—only the majority: seven out of the thirteen or more. The moment that you start describing your hand to your partner, you will promise that your side will make seven tricks or more. The more you describe what you have, the higher the level will get and the more tricks you will have to make. So, for that reason, you cannot start the auction for your side without 12 high card points. In this way, you have a little over the average number of points (10) so that on average you and your partner will hold the majority of points.

Do not worry if you promise to make seven tricks by starting the bidding and your partner has nothing. Your opponents will soon be in the auction themselves and you will not be left having to make all those tricks on your own (it does happen occasionally but not very often).

Your partner will then tell you roughly how many points he holds and you will then try to find out the two key things from the auction:

- How many points you have between you—to decide how many tricks/which level to bid to.
- In which suit (if any) you hold eight cards between your two hands—to decide which suit will be trumps or whether you play in no-trumps.

This will allow you to decide whether to aim for a part-score (a contract which scores part of a game), or whether to go for the game contract (which scores your side 100pts or more below the line).

An Example

Let's look at a simple hand, based upon the very little we know so far about the bidding. The person who deals the cards has the first chance to speak. If his hand contains fewer than 12 points, he cannot start the bidding for his side, so he says "No-bid" or "Pass." It doesn't matter which you say, just stick to the same word/phrase throughout or your opponents may suspect you of cheating.

The bidding then moves in a clockwise direction around the table. If no one has 12pts or more, then everyone may say "No-bid" and the hand would be thrown-in and the next person would deal a hand. This does not happen often, but it does occur.

Let's assume that at your table, your opponents are saying "No-bid," and these are your hands:

partner
♠ KQ85
♥ Q3
♦ K643
♣ Q64

```
      N
  W       E
      S
```

you
♠ A7432
♥ AK85
♦ A2
♣ 73

Let's imagine that East (one of your opponents) was the dealer and he says "No-bid"—meaning that he has fewer than 12pts in his hand. It is now your turn to bid (as South) and, with 15pts, you are going to open the bidding to tell your partner you have 12pts or more, and which suit in your hand contains the most cards. You'll say: "1 Spade." All everyone knows about your hand so far is that you hold 12pts or more—to start the bidding—and at least a 4-card spade suit, because you never suggest a suit for trumps unless you hold at least four cards in it.

What does "1 Spade"—or "1S" as it would appear in a bidding chart—actually mean? If all three remaining players now said "No-bid," it's like an auction with the auctioneer saying "Going...Going...Gone!" If there is a bid at bridge and then the next three people say "No-bid," then that is the end of the auction and whatever was last said becomes the contract.

So, if West, North, and East all said "No-bid" now, the contract would be 1 Spade. That is to say, North-South would have to try to make seven tricks (the six we take for granted plus the one we have bid) with spades as trumps.

This happens only very rarely because your partner almost always responds to your opening bid, or your opponents get involved in the auction.

Here, West (your other opponent) says "No-bid," and your partner North says to himself something like this: "My partner has 12pts or more and I have 12pts...that gives us at least 24pts...looking at my chart on page 18, and remembering that, for suit contracts, it is only a rough guide, I can see that we are safe to play at the 2- or maybe 3-level. Probably the higher level, because I know we have a fit (that is to say, we have at least eight spades between us to have as a trump suit). So, I want to tell my partner that I like spades as the trump suit, and that we have enough points to make eight or nine tricks if he is minimum and, if he has a few extra points we might go for 4 Spades—ten tricks—which would score us game all in one go if my partner can make the tricks."

So the correct bid for North to make now would be to jump to 3 Spades. When East says "No-bid" again, you as South will reason that if your partner thinks your side could make nine tricks if you only held 12pts then, as you hold 15pts, going for the game contract must be worth it, so you bid 4 Spades.

If we were looking at this auction in a bidding chart, this is how it would look:

N	E	S	W	Dealer East
—	NB	1S	NB	
3S	NB	4S	all pass	

If you follow the reasoning of this auction, you are doing incredibly well, because we leapt ahead a bit there. This auction would not disgrace the world championships, so well done if you are following so far.

This auction had one big advantage—North-South knew straightaway which suit was going to be trumps. That meant your only decision was how many tricks to go for....With 27pts between you, you opted to go for ten tricks in a contract of 4 Spades—which, if made, would score you 120pts below the line and a game contract.

Try Another Hand

partner
♠ KQ8
♥ Q3
♦ K6432
♣ J64

you
♠ A7432
♥ AK85
♦ A7
♣ 73

The hands here are almost the same but, this time, when you as South open the bidding with 1 Spade, North can only assume that you hold a 4-card suit and so, with 3-card spade support, he cannot agree to have that suit as trumps yet, because he is not sure that there are eight trumps between the two hands. So, when it comes to North's turn to bid, he will suggest an alternative suit as trumps and wait to hear what else you tell him about your hand.

Let's see what happens. With your opponents (East-West) saying "No-bid" throughout, you as South open the bidding with 1 Spade—promising 12pts or more and four or more spades. North now wants to show his 5-card diamond suit. Can he bid 1 Diamond?

The key is the order of suits we looked at first on page 6. You will remember they ran as follows:

NT	no-trumps
♠	spades
♥	hearts
♦	diamonds
♣	clubs

The way the auction works is this: If you want to bid a suit that is higher-ranking (higher up on the list as shown) than the last bid made, you can do this at the same level. That is to say, if your partner bids 1 Club, you could say "1 Diamond," "1 Heart," "1 Spade," or "1NT," because all those suits are higher in the list than clubs. But, if partner bids 1 Spade, then if you want to bid diamonds, you will have to say "2 Diamonds," because diamonds are lower ranking on the list than spades. In this way, you can see that the auction can escalate quite quickly and that is why you must be careful not to get too high for the number of points you have in your hand. We will see how to avoid this and to bid well in the forthcoming chapter.

So, in this example, North will have to bid 2 Diamonds because diamonds are less important in the list than spades. North's bid is what we call a response—replying to partner's opening bid. For this reason, North requires fewer than the 12pts you need to open the bidding for your side because his partner has already promised an opening hand. Exact point-counts for responses will be discussed a bit later.

Having suggested spades originally, you as South now show that you have four hearts in your hand as well, and you do this by bidding 2 Hearts. You can bid hearts at the same level because they are a higher-ranking suit than diamonds. For reasons that are explained in full on page 61, this bid now shows that you hold five spades and at least four hearts so, now, North knows that your side holds eight spades between you and that they can be trumps. With 11pts in his hand opposite your minimum of 12pts, he decides to support spades and to jump a level to show he holds extra points, so he bids 3 Spades. Like last time you—with 15pts rather than the 12pts you might have held—decide to bid on to 4 Spades, which would give your side game. The bidding chart would look like this.

N	E	S	W	Dealer South
—	NB	1S	NB	
2D	NB	2H	NB	
3S	NB	4S	all pass	

Why each bid means something must be learned and understood slowly and over time. You cannot learn bridge quickly—it's impossible. So far, you have seen the basic outline of the game and the way that the game operates. In the next chapter, we will look at some specifics of bidding, and then move on to the play of the cards.

PART TWO

The Bidding

6

The Positions at the Table

Before we look at certain bids in detail, it is worth pointing out a key element of the bidding. Once someone opens the bidding for his side, everyone else at the table has roles that, for the duration of the hand, are cast in stone. Let me show you what I mean:

Dealer South

	♠ KJ76	
	♥ 103	
	♦ KJ108	
	♣ J104	
♠ A3		♠ 84
♥ KQJ865	N / W E / S	♥ A72
♦ Q75		♦ 432
♣ 73		♣ AKQ85
	♠ Q10952	
	♥ 94	
	♦ A96	
	♣ 962	

The dealer is South, so he gets the first chance to speak. He holds only 6pts, so he cannot open the bidding. He says, "No-bid." The bidding moves clockwise and it is West to speak next. He does hold 12pts and a nice long suit too, so he opens "1 Heart."

For the duration of this hand, everyone now has roles:

West is the Opener—he made the opening bid.

East is the Responder—he is the partner of the opener.

North and South are the Overcallers—they are the opponents who may, at some stage decide to "call over" (hence overcall) the opening bid in an attempt to steal the contract or interfere with the bidding of East and West.

What is the significance of these roles?

Each bid in bridge means something different depending upon the position in which it is made. Simply:

- **An opening bid** of 1 Spade means that you have at least four spades and 12pts or more.
- If your partner has opened the bidding with, say, 1 Diamond, and you **in response** bid 1 Spade, this also shows at least four spades, but a different point-count.
- If your opponent has opened the bidding and you want to **overcall** 1 Spade, then this bid promises a five card spade suit and another different point-count.

So, the language is simple, but the context of each bid is vital and quite tough to master. Oh, by the way, that IS the game...and it takes a lifetime to realize you will never master it totally.

So, now, let's get under way with some of the bidding.

7

Opening and Responding to 1NT

This is the first bid we will look at because it is the opening bid that you will make most often. As we have discussed before, when you have a balanced hand, to begin with at least you are thinking of playing the contract in no-trumps (without a trump suit).

Opening 1NT

An opening bid of 1NT shows a balanced distribution with exactly 12, 13 or 14pts.

Never 11, never 15! If you hold more than 14pts, you will have to open your best suit and then bid no-trumps later on. Players in some countries play that an opening bid of 1NT shows a different point-count; in the UK a "Weak No-trump" is played and that shows 12–14pts. The good news is that once you have made this bid, the main decision-making on this hand will be up to your partner, because you have described what you have in your hand, almost completely. Let's see some examples:

a) ♠ A974   b) ♠ K54   c) ♠ 865
    ♥ AK85   ♥ Q73   ♥ AJ864
    ♦ Q62   ♦ J6   ♦ KJ7
    ♣ J7   ♣ AQJ96   ♣ A9

a) 1NT. It is a balanced hand (no more than eight cards between your two longest suits) with 14pts so this is perfect to open with 1NT. The fact that you have only two clubs is irrelevant: with 12–14pts you can't have great cards in every suit.

b) 1NT. Again, a balanced hand. You do hold a good quality 5-card club suit but, because it is a minor suit, you would far prefer to play in a no-trump contract than with clubs as trumps (because of the scoring and the number of tricks you require to make game—see page 24).

c) Here you do not open 1NT, but instead 1 Heart. It may be a balanced hand but it contains a 5-card major suit. Because playing with a major suit as trumps is slightly preferable to playing in no-trumps, it is better to open one-of-a-major rather than 1NT when you hold five cards in hearts or spades.

That's it. The most common opening bid in bridge and that's it covered. It's worth adding that, because you have described your hand pretty accurately, once you have opened 1NT you never bid again unless your partner, by his response, asks you a specific question.

Responding to 1NT

Responding to 1NT becomes very simple as you get used to the principles involved. For now, keep looking at your point-chart on page 18, and remember that, if game is in your sights, these are your targets:

4 Hearts or 4 Spades

Making ten tricks in hearts or spades—with at least eight trumps between you—is usually the best way to score game.

3 No-trumps

In very close second, nine tricks in no-trumps is an excellent way to score game.

5 Clubs or 5 Diamonds

Miles below the other two, eleven tricks in clubs or diamonds is a long haul to score a game contract.

For this reason, when you hold a long minor suit, your thoughts are often on playing in no-trumps (where your long suit will prove very useful) rather than trying to make so many tricks in 5 Clubs or 5 Diamonds.

When your partner opens 1NT, you know immediately that he has a balanced hand, with no singletons (suits containing only one card) or voids (suits with no cards in them). For this reason you should be able to judge with what to respond with relative ease.

Responding with Balanced Hands or a Distributional Hand with a Long Minor Suit

Let's start with supporting partner in no-trumps, on hands where we have a balanced hand (or a distributional hand containing a long minor suit—as we would rather play in 3NT than 5 Clubs or 5 Diamonds). This is just a matter of arithmetic—referring to our level chart on page 18 again.

With 0–10pts, we have a minimum of 12pts between us and a maximum of 24. However good or bad that total may be, there is no chance of bidding 3NT—which is the game contract. So, we should say **"No-bid."**

With 11 or 12pts, we should think as follows: If partner has 12pts (a minimum 1NT opener) then we have 23 or 24pts between us and that is safe for 2NT. If he holds a maximum 1NT opener (14pts) then we have 25 or 26pts between us, which is enough for a game contract. Bid **2NT**—this asks the opener to pass if he is minimum, and to bid on to 3NT if he is maximum. (If he has 13pts, he will have to agonize over what to do!)

With 13pts or more, we should reason: Partner has a minimum of 12pts and I have 13pts. That makes 25pts and that is enough for game. Bid **3NT** immediately.

To summarize, with a balanced hand opposite a 1NT Opener:

0–10pts   No-bid
11–12pts 2NT—inviting partner to bid 3NT if maximum
13pts+   3NT

Now try these examples:

a) ♠ KJ8   b) ♠ K54   c) ♠ Q86
    ♥ AQ5   ♥ Q732   ♥ J8
    ♦ Q642   ♦ J632   ♦ K7
    ♣ J73   ♣ A9   ♣ AJ9542

a)   3NT. Opposite partner's 1NT opener, you have a minimum of 25pts between you (12 in partner's hand, 13 in yours). So, try to score game all in one go.

b)   No-bid. A very nice hand, and a maximum pass. However, since you do not hold enough points to make game a possibility, it is better to leave partner playing in a low part-score than risk getting too high.

c)   3NT. Although you do not have a balanced hand, with your long minor suit, you are worth a punt at scoring game. With a long minor suit it is almost always better to support no-trumps than to bid the minor suit, as you don't want to play in 5C or 5D. Secondly, you can add 1pt to your total for every card over 4 in your long suit so, here, you can add 2pts to your 11 to make a hand worth 13pts, and therefore 3NT. This is a risky bid and it will go wrong sometimes, but it is a big winner in the long run.

So, you have two golden rules to think about:

•   With minor suits, do not bid those suits in response to 1NT, just support no-trumps.
•   When bidding no-trumps, add 1pt to your total for each card over 4 in your long suit.

Responding with Other Distributional Hands

When you have a long major suit, or an extra weak hand, there are other responses to be made. Let's start with the good news: the game-going hands.

These are hands on which you have an opening hand yourself and your partner opens the bidding with 1NT ahead of you. As a rule, if you have a hand on which you would have opened the bidding (12pts or more) and your partner has opened the bidding, you should usually head for a game contract. Remember that, basically:

- An opening hand opposite an opening hand equals game.

So, with the opponents saying "No-bid" throughout, your partner opens 1NT and this is your hand:

♠ AJ7532
♥ A63
♦ AJ2
♣ 9

This is the way you should think when deciding what to bid:

Combining Points and Level
Your partner has a minimum of 12pts and you hold 14pts, so you have at least 26pts between you as a partnership. You also have a long suit, which improves your hand, so you should think that you have a game contract available to you.

Finding a Fit
If you hold eight cards or more between you and your partner in the same suit, this is a fit. This is what you are seeking as, with a fit, you know which suit will be trumps. Now, you merely have to decide the correct level.

Look first for an 8-card fit in a major suit (hearts and spades), then for a possible no-trump contract and finally, only if there is no alternative, think about playing in a minor suit (diamonds or clubs) contract.

Here, you hold a 6-card spade suit, and your partner,

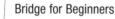

who promised a balanced hand with his 1NT opener, must hold at least two spades. So, you have an 8-card fit in spades, so that suit will be trumps.

Putting It Together

Your partnership has enough points for game, and you know that you have eight spades between you. Therefore, make haste...Bid now to a game contract with spades as trumps: 4 Spades.

Often in bridge, you and your partner will have a lengthy conversation about the level and trump suit in which you will play. But, opposite a 1NT opening, the partner of the opener usually makes the decision pretty quickly.

Compare the above example with this one:

Again, with the opponents saying "No-bid" throughout, your partner opens 1NT and this is your hand:

♠ J2
♥ A63
♦ A2
♣ AJ7542

It is quite similar to the previous example except this time your long suit is clubs—a minor suit. As you want to avoid playing in 5 Clubs or 5 Diamonds—it is SO many tricks to have to make—you should play in no-trumps instead and respond 3NT immediately. It is a small risk, as your opponents may be able to take too many spade tricks quickly, but it is your best chance of scoring game.

Let's take a look at this hand:

♠ KQ963
♥ A63
♦ AJ2
♣ 74

Here, your partner opens 1NT and your opponents say "No-bid" throughout. What should you respond?

In order to let the 1NT opener know that you have an opening hand and that you want to go to game, you need to jump a level—this tells him that you are strong. You cannot bid 4 Spades directly because you only hold five spades and partner may only hold two spades and then you would not have your desired 8-card fit. So, you should consult partner over the final contract by bidding 3 Spades.

By jumping to 3 Spades, this tells the 1NT opener that you want to be in game. However, he can work out that if you had held a 6-card suit you would have jumped to 4 Spades, so you are showing a 5-card spade suit and a desire to be in game. We call this type of bid "forcing," because partner is forced to bid again:

If he holds three spades or more opposite your 5-card suit, he bids 4 Spades—knowing that you have an 8-card fit and points for game.

If he holds only a doubleton spade (2-card suit), then he will know that you do not hold the desired 8-card fit, and he rebids 3NT.

This auction would be exactly the same if hearts had been your suit. But if you had held this type of hand with clubs or diamonds, you would have ignored the suit and supported no-trumps, bidding 3NT directly here.

You would never bid a 4-card suit opposite 1NT because if you held only a 4-card suit, your hand would be balanced and you would be supporting no-trumps (as detailed on page 48).

The Weak Take-Out

What happens when you have a weaker hand?

With 0–11pts and a long suit, it is vital that you do not switch off and leave your partner to suffer in a horrible contract. Take this hand, where your partner has opened 1NT and your opponents are passing:

♠ J97532
♥ 6
♦ 8532
♣ 52

Your instinct may tell you to say "No-bid" quickly but you must think more carefully. Your partner holds a maximum of 14pts and you have 1pt so your opponents are in good shape. They may enter the bidding and steal the contract, perhaps even reaching game (they do have 25–27pts between them, after all).

However, they may find it difficult to get into the auction as they would have to bid at the 2-level and will require a long suit (see Overcalls, page 82) so they may decide to leave your partner to suffer in 1NT. Clearly, your hand is so weak, with two marked shortages, that a 1NT contract will be a disaster. Can you see a less horrendous contract? Whatever you bid will involve you being too high for your combined point-count, but you are in a damage-limitation situation here. Your 6-card spade suit will provide tricks only if you play in spades, where those cards can be used for trumping. So, you should bid 2 Spades.

Any bid at the 2-level, in response to an opening bid of 1NT, is called a "Weak Take-out." You are so weak that you are taking your partner out of 1NT and into the less disastrous contract of 2-of-a-suit. The 1NT opener never ever…ever…ever bids again after a Weak Take-out…Ever!! This is because you may have as few as zero points and still feel the need to rescue your partner.

I would anticipate that a 1NT contract would fail by about four tricks, whereas a 2 Spade contract would fail by only two tricks. Both are failures, but you have managed to limit your losses.

Let's recap the main responses to a 1NT opener:

BRIEFING

Responding to 1NT

Balanced Hands

0–10pts	No-bid.	
11–12pts	2NT.	Inviting opener to bid 3NT if maximum.
13pts+	3NT.	

Distributional Hands

0–11pts	Weak Take-out: bid your 5-card suit at the 2-level: Opener always passes.
12pts+	5-card major suit: bid 3H or 3S (forcing bid). Opener bids 3NT with 2-card support or 4H/4S with 3-card support.
	6-card major suit: bid 4H or 4S. Opener always passes.
	Long minor suits—always support no-trumps.

You will find that you see 1NT opened frequently and that you are soon able to practice the basic responses. Glance at this chart when you have a problem, but you will soon find that you can work out the correct bid in quicker and quicker time as you get used to the game.

8
Opening and Responding
to 1-of-a-Suit

The bidding in bridge is about telling your partner what you have in your hand so that you, as a partnership, can decide on the best contract for your side. Your sources of information are quite limited, but the most informative area of the auction is the opening bid and then the opener's second bid, which is called the "opener's rebid." In these two bids, you learn both the shape and point-count of the opener's hand quite accurately and this will allow you to make a good decision as responder.

First, let's glance at the responder's hand and look at two basic responses:

When your partner opens 1 Club, 1 Diamond, 1 Heart, or 1 Spade, you can count on him for 12pts or more, up to a maximum of about 20pts (with more than this he would probably open the bidding with a different first bid, possibly at the 2-level—but this is very rare).

For this reason, in the responding position when you hold 6pts or more, you need to make a bid. Partner could hold 20pts and your 6pts would make a partnership total of 26pts—enough for a game contract—an opportunity you would not wish to miss.

To respond at the 1-level, you only need 6pts or more.

If the auction involves you having to bid at the 2-level, then you require a minimum of 8pts, because you have moved up a level and promised to make more tricks.

To respond at the 2-level (without jumping) you need 8pts or more.

If you, as responder, change the suit, the opener MUST make a second bid (rebid) to keep the auction going, so there is no chance of him suddenly passing and leaving you to play in whatever you just bid.

We will return to the responder's bids in the next section but, with this basic background, we can fit together many more pieces of this seemingly very difficult puzzle.

Opening Bids and Rebids with Balanced Hands

With what do you open the bidding with each of these hands?

a) ♠ A63
♥ Q95
♦ AJ742
♣ Q3

b) ♠ AK53
♥ Q962
♦ KJ7
♣ K9

c) ♠ K86
♥ AKJ
♦ K7
♣ AJ954

a) **1NT.** It is a balanced hand with 12–14pts and that means that we must open the bidding with 1NT.

b) **1 Heart.** It is a balanced hand, so you will want to bid no-trumps. However, with 16pts, you are far too strong to start the auction with 1NT. So, you must start with one of your 4-card suits and then rebid no-trumps next time.

With two 4-card suits and too many points to open 1NT, bid hearts if you have them or otherwise the lower ranking of your two 4-card suits. This ensures that you find your major suit fit if you have one and keep the bidding low if you do not. The relative quality of the suits is irrelevant and should never influence you as to which suit to open.

c) **1 Club.** Again, you have a balanced hand with too many points to open 1NT. So, open 1 Club, and when partner responds, you can then rebid no-trumps.

How do you know how many no-trumps to rebid? It is a matter of arithmetic. This is part of the chart on page 18.

pts between the partnership	number of tricks	level
20–22	7 tricks likely	1-level
23–24	8 tricks likely	2-level
25–26	9 tricks likely	3-level

This is hand b) from the examples above:

♠ AK53
♥ Q962
♦ KJ7
♣ K9

You open the bidding with **1 Heart**. Remembering that an 8-card fit in a major suit is your top priority, if your partner supports hearts, that will be your contract; if he bids spades, you will support him.

If, however, he bids 2 Clubs, you, with your balanced hand, must rebid NTs to show him your balanced shape and your point-count. All you do now is to add your points to the points your partner has shown and bid the appropriate number of NTs. Here, your partner has changed the suit at the 2-level, promising a minimum of 8pts and you hold 16pts. Add these together to make a combined total of 24pts and, as you can see from the chart you are safe to bid at the 2-level, so you rebid 2NT. If your partner is stronger than 8pts, he can bid on, raising you to 3NT with a balanced hand or continuing to describe the shape of his own hand by bidding other suits. The key is that you have shown your partner a balanced hand with an exact point-count and that should allow him to judge the final contract quite accurately.

Let's see some examples of auctions:

1C—1H

1NT   Your 1NT rebid shows a balanced hand with too many points to have opened 1NT. As partner has promised only 6pts to respond at the 1-level, you must hold **15–16pts** to give you a partnership total of 21–22pts.

1C—1H

2NT   Your 2NT rebid shows **17–18pts** which, added to the 6pts or more your partner holds, gives your side a minimum of 23 or 24pts between you: perfect for 2NT.

1C—1H

3NT   Your 3NT rebid shows **19–20pts** as, opposite as few as 6pts in partner's hand, you must have the remaining points to give you a partnership total of 25–26pts.

1S—2C

2NT   Partner has responded at the 2-level promising at least 8pts, so your rebid shows **15 or 16pts.** 8 plus 15–16 gives you 23 or 24pts—putting you at the correct level.

1S—2C

3NT   Your 3NT rebid shows 17–20pts. You may have as few as 17pts because, since your partner could bid at the 2-level, he must have at least 8pts and 8 + 17 = 25pts—enough for a game contract.

In each case, if the responder holds only the minimum point-count for his response, he can pass, leaving you in a sensible contract.

If, on the other hand, he holds more points than he has shown, he can bid on, either supporting you or continuing to describe his hand by bidding new suits.

By opening 1NT or, if you have 15pts or more, opening 1-of-a-suit and then rebidding no-trumps, you are showing a balanced hand. If, as opener, you fail to bid no-trumps either as an opening bid or as a rebid, then you are denying a balanced hand and your partner will know that your hand shape is distributional.

Opening Bids and Rebids with Distributional Hands

A distributional hand contains nine or more cards between your two longest suits.

When this is the case, you should not suggest a no-trump contract early on in the auction as, for the moment, you are thinking about having one of your long suits as a trump suit. Your side may end up in no-trumps if you fail to find an 8-card fit or if you decide to play in no-trumps rather than a minor suit, but you must describe your hand early on in the bidding process. Let's see some examples:

♠ KJ974
♥ AQ96
♦ AJ5
♣ 6

This is not a balanced hand: you have nine cards between your two longest suits (spades and hearts) and a singleton club.

You always open your longest suit, regardless of quality.

So, you open 1 Spade—promising 12pts or more and a 4-card spade suit—and your partner responds 2 Clubs. This is not great news—because your partner is bidding a suit you hate, but at least you know that he holds 8pts or more because he responded at the 2-level (see page 56). So, your 15pts and his minimum of 8pts means that you have at least 23pts between you and you are still at a safe level.

You now rebid your second suit—hearts—and the auction looks like this:

you	partner
1S	2C
2H	

Your partner now knows that you hold two biddable suits, but he knows something further too. You hold at least five spades and at least four hearts. How does he know this?

If you had held just four spades and four hearts, you would have a balanced hand (no more than eight cards between your two longest suits) and you would either have opened 1NT (with 12–14pts) or, with more points, opened a suit and then rebid no-trumps to show your balanced hand. Because you have failed to bid no-trumps as an opening bid or a rebid, you must have a distributional hand containing at least nine cards between your two longest suits.

Partner knows that you have at least five spades, because you always open your longest suit first, regardless of quality.

If, as opener or responder, you bid two different suits, you promise at least five cards in the first suit and four cards in the second.

As opener, you never—ever—bid two 4-card suits. If that were your hand, you would have a balanced hand and you would either open 1NT, or bid one of your suits and then rebid no-trumps.

Let's see how we can use that information to develop an auction:

Here's your hand again and now you can see your partner's hand too.

you	partner
♠ KJ974	♠ AQ6
♥ AQ96	♥ K5
♦ AJ5	♦ 842
♣ 6	♣ A9752

you	partner
1S	2C
2H	?

What should your partner bid now? Partner should think like this:

My partner has an opening hand and so do I. At the end of the auction our side should be in game. (An opening hand opposite an opening hand equals game.)

My partner originally showed me a 4-card spade suit but now that he has bid a second suit, I know that he is at least 5–4 in those two suits. If he has five spades then, with my 3-card support, we have an 8-card fit in spades, and that suit should be trumps. I know we should be in game, and I know that spades should be trumps...what am I waiting for?

Partner bids 4 Spades—getting your side to the correct game contract.

Let's look at another example:

♠ 85
♥ AQJ985
♦ AQ7
♣ 63

Again, this is a distributional hand, this time with only one long suit to bid. You are going to open the bidding with 1H and then bid hearts again.

As opener:

- If you bid a suit once, you promise a 4-card suit or longer.
- If you bid a suit twice, you promise a 5-card suit or longer.
- If you bid a suit three times, you promise a 6-card suit or longer.

If you have to bid a third time, you will bid hearts again to show a 6-card suit. Let's look at partner's hand too and plot the auction.

you	partner
♠ 85	♠ AQ764
♥ AQJ985	♥ K3
♦ AQ7	♦ K642
♣ 63	♣ 72

1H	1S
2H	3D
3H	?

You open 1 Heart and your partner responds 1 Spade. This only promises a 4-card spade suit and 6pts or more. You dutifully rebid your heart suit—promising at least a 5-card suit. Now, your partner bids a second suit of his own. This promises that he holds at least five spades and four diamonds. It also promises that he has a good hand because he has bid at the 3-level when you have promised no more than 12pts and because every time the responder changes the suit, the opener is forced to keep bidding.

You bid 3 Hearts, promising a 6-card suit…What does your partner say now?

This is how he should reason:

My partner has shown me a hand with a 6-card hearts suit. As I have 2-card heart support for him and he has promised a 6-card suit, I know we have an 8-card fit in hearts, so that suit should be trumps. I have an opening hand opposite an opening hand, so we should be in game. So, I will bid 4 Hearts.

Once again, simple bidding and good thinking has got your side to its best game contract. Notice that 3NT is a terrible contract to be in because you have no high cards in clubs in either hand and your opponents will be able to reel off tricks there without you having any means by which to stop them.

Finally, look at this example:

you	partner
♠ 85	♠ AK742
♥ AQ865	♥ K3
♦ J7	♦ AQ85
♣ AK63	♣ 72
1H	1S
2C	?

You have opened with 1 Heart and after partner's 1 Spade response, you have correctly rebid 2 Clubs. This shows at least five hearts and four clubs. But what should your partner bid now?

This is how he should think:

I have an opening hand opposite an opening hand, so our side should end up in a game contract. My partner has five hearts and four clubs and does not seem interested in my spades. We may have an 8-card fit in spades, but we are running out of time to investigate. Since I have excellent spades and diamonds and partner has hearts and clubs and we do not seem to have an 8-card fit in a major suit (hearts or spades) I will opt to play without a trump suit in no-trumps.

So, partner should bid 3NT, because with his 16pts and your 12pts or more, he knows that you have at least 28pts between you. He does not need to bid more than 3NT, because 3NT scores 100pts and game and there is no point in bidding any higher.

9

Supporting Partner

The best news partner can hear is when you support his suit and decide that it should be trumps. Now, all that is left is to decide the level at which to play. Generally, if you are looking for game, you will try to play in a major suit fit (hearts or spades) or in 3NT. Playing in 5 Clubs or 5 Diamonds is not a good idea, unless you have no choice.

In simple terms, the moment you know that you and your partner have an 8-card fit in hearts or spades, you should support him—and take him as high as you think your side can make, based on the bidding so far.

Bridge is a game that is often about making the best of bad news, but let's see some good news:

Your partner opens 1 Heart. What should you respond on these hands?

a) ♠ 3
    ♥ K953
    ♦ J854
    ♣ K982

b) ♠ 64
    ♥ KJ83
    ♦ A732
    ♣ K43

c) ♠ 86
    ♥ KJ753
    ♦ 3
    ♣ KQ754

a) **2 Hearts.** This "simple raise" shows 6–9pts and usually 4-card support (rarely, 3-card support also—see d) below).

    Opener only bids on if he holds a very strong hand.

b) **3 Hearts.** This "jump-raise" shows 4-card support and 10–12pts. It invites the opener to bid on to game if he has a little more than he promised initially. It says: "I nearly have an opening hand opposite an opening hand, so I am nearly bidding game."

c) **4 Hearts.** This looks a little odd. You only hold 9pts after all, but look at the shape of the hand. You have 5-card trump support, two useful shortages, and a second suit that will make tricks. This bid really has two purposes: first to get you to a likely making-game contract; second, to keep your opponents out of the auction. They probably hold spades and might enter the auction if you just bid a meager 2 Hearts.

    An immediate jump to game (1 Heart–4 Hearts or 1 Spade–4 Spades) shows a weak hand in terms of points (0–9pts) but a strong hand in terms of distribution.

Points for Distribution

Most bridge players add on points for distribution when they hold distributional hands. You should only do this once you know for certain which suit will be trumps. You should also only add these points on if your partner has not bid the suit (if the opponents have bid it, that's fine—add on the points!). Then when you are about to support your partner, you can add the following bonuses to your hand:

For a doubleton	add 1pt.
For a singleton	add 3pts.
For a void	add 5pts.

Please remember—only add these points to your hand when you are about to support your partner's suit.

So, if you look at hand c) again, it may contain only 9 high card points, but you can add 4pts on to that total (1pt for your doubleton spade; 3pts for your singleton diamond) and that makes it up to the equivalent of 13pts.

Partner still opens 1 Heart: what do you respond?

d)
- ♠ 963
- ♥ K95
- ♦ J2
- ♣ Q9842

e)
- ♠ AQ6
- ♥ KJ83
- ♦ 72
- ♣ A853

d) **2 Hearts.** Although you only hold 3-card heart support, partner often holds a 5-card suit when he opens, so this will usually be the correct trump suit. With weak hands of 6–8pts, supporting partner with three trumps is preferable to a response of 1NT (see page 71). As your raise may only show 3-card support, partner will not bid any higher in hearts without at least a 5-card suit.

Any time that you support a minor suit, it promises 4-card support.

e)   **4 Hearts.** This is the only time I lie to you (to protect you, of course). This is not the best bid (you will remember the correct meaning of this jump to game is a weak hand with 0–9pts and good distribution) but the correct bid requires deeper knowledge than you yet have. This will, at least, get you to the correct spot most of the time (opening hand opposite opening hand; 8-card heart fit—it can't be bad!).

Support a major suit as trumps the moment you know that you have an 8-card fit.

1H—2H Shows 6–9pts and 3- or 4-card support.
1H—3H Shows 10–12pts and 4-card support.
1H—4H Shows 0–9pts with excellent support and distribution (for the moment, too, it shows hands of 13pts or more with 4-card support).

All raises of minor suits guarantee 4-card support and deny a 4-card major suit in your hand, which you would always show ahead of supporting a minor suit—or anything else!

10

Responding with 1NT

As responder, you sometimes have a balanced hand on which you wish to bid no-trumps. Generally, responding with no-trumps straightaway is a bad idea—you can end up in no-trumps later but it is usually better to describe your hand first. However, there is one very important no-trump response and that is 1NT.

Your partner opens 1 Diamond. What should you respond on each of these hands?

a)   ♠ Q963   b)   ♠ AQ6   c)   ♠ Q86
       ♥ K95   ♥ KJ8   ♥ K75
       ♦ J2   ♦ 732   ♦ 853
       ♣ AK98   ♣ K943   ♣ Q754

a)   **1 Spade.** Responder's top priority is to show any 4-card spade or heart suit at the 1-level regardless of quality. With this hand, your side will end up in game, and you must check if there is a 4–4 fit in spades before anything else.

b) **2 Clubs.** You could bid 3NT straightaway. You have a balanced hand with 13pts so game in no-trumps is a good shot. But, it is better to change the suit—which forces the opener to bid again—so that you can learn more about his hand before deciding in which game contract to play.

c) **1NT.** You have 7pts so you need to respond in case your partner holds a very strong hand. You cannot bid at the 2-level, because you do not hold 8pts (see page 56). The only 1-level bid you can make therefore is 1NT. This shows a weak hand with usually 6–8, sometimes 9pts, on which you need to say something, but do not wish to bid at the 2-level.

Opposite that response of 1NT, the opener knows that you are weak, and limited to an absolute maximum of 9pts. He will not get overexcited. Unlike almost all other no-trump bids, a response of 1NT does not show a balanced hand. It is merely the cheapest bid available to show partner a few points, but insufficient strength to bid anything else.

When you respond 1NT opposite a major suit opening (1 Heart or 1 Spade), you show a marked dislike for your partner's suit.

Partner opens 1 Heart:

a)   ♠ K86   b) ♠ 963   c) ♠ Q86
        ♥ 5   ♥ −   ♥ K75
        ♦ J9642   ♦ 8732   ♦ J97532
        ♣ K983   ♣ KQJ943   ♣ 4

a)   **1NT.** You have 7pts, so you want to bid something. You are not strong enough to bid 2 Diamonds, so staying at the 1-level is wise.

b)   **1NT**. Again, not enough points to bid at the 2-level despite your nice 6-card suit. Respond 1NT and, if opener bids hearts again, now you bid clubs. He can work out that you must have lots of clubs, but very few points, and he should then pass.

c)   **2 Hearts.** If you respond 1NT to a 1 Heart or 1 Spade opening bid, you deny 3-card support or better for partner's suit. This is because with a weak hand it is usually better to support a major suit with 3-card support than to bid 1NT. Here, with your singleton club and three decent hearts, 2 Hearts looks a better spot than 1NT.

     Indeed, opposite a 1 Heart or 1 Spade opening bid, a response of 1NT denies 3-card support for the major suit and shows a weak hand. A 1NT response need not show a balanced hand—it is a bid that warns the opener that you are only just worth a response.

11
Competitive Bidding:
Doubles and Overcalls

Up until now, you and your partner have been allowed to communicate uninterrupted. There is a simple logic to, at least, some of the bidding. However, one of the great elements of bridge is that you can interfere with your opponents' bidding, even if you have quite a weak hand, in order to impede their progress to the correct contract. Your aim when competing is primarily to disrupt, harass, upset, and disorientate your opponents: it's the point at which bridge turns from being a gentle game into war!

Once your opponent has opened the bidding, everyone's roles are cast in stone for the duration of the hand (see page 43). Your side is "the overcallers." You may end up stealing the contract, or you may simply enter the auction to cause trouble. Whatever the reason, it is essential that you compete safely and effectively. The good news is that, whatever variations of the bidding language are played globally, almost everyone competes in the same way.

There are two ways to compete. One is to use a new bid "Double"; the other to "overcall"—that is to say, to bid your own long suit while your opponents are bidding. We will look at both in turn, starting with the stronger maneuver: Double.

Double

First, a brief history lesson.

Double is a bid that has been around since modern bridge began. Traditionally, it was used when your opponents reached a contract you were convinced that they could not make. To punish them and to gain extra penalty points, you "doubled" the final contract. If your opponents succeeded, they got double points; if they failed, you got extra penalty points (actually quite a bit more than double points). That was the only use for the bid. In time, the bid "Redouble" appeared. This bid was traditionally made by the player you had doubled if he was certain he could make his contract. If he did make it, he got four times the points; if he failed, you got more than four times the penalty points. It was not a bid that saw much action and today, "Redouble" is really only used in other situations. To see how penalty points are scored, see page 155.

At least you have now met all thirty-eight of the bridge bids that exist:

1C through to 7NT—that's thirty-five possible bids.
Double and Redouble.
Pass or No-bid.

That's it—there are no more terms lurking anywhere—
that is your complete vocabulary.

Take-out Double

Because Double was really only used at quite high levels,
bridge innovators decided that it was a pity to waste the bid
at lower levels, and so they invented the Take-out Double.
If you use the bid Double now, it is not usually intended to
try to penalize your opponents; it is used to ask your partner to bid. Let's see an example. Your right hand opponent
opens the bidding with 1 Diamond and you hold this hand.
What can you bid?

♠ AQ85
♥ KJ74
♦ 8
♣ K752

As we will see when we look at Overcalls next, in order to
bid a suit once an opponent has opened the bidding you
must hold a 5-card suit. Here, however, there is an excellent alternative, and that is to say "Double."

This says the following things to partner:

- I have an opening hand (12pts or more).
- I have a shortage in the suit the opponent has bid—
  not more than two cards…ever.
- I guarantee 3-card support (more often, 4-card support) for every one of the unbid suits.

When it is your partner's turn to bid, he will then take you
out of the Double by choosing one of those remaining suits
and you will, all being well, find your fit. This cancels
the Double.

The Take-out Double always shows your partner a choice of suits from which he must choose and can be used after your opponents have bid just one suit or after they have bid two different suits.

Your left hand opponent opens 1 Diamond, your partner passes, and your right hand opponent bids 1 Spade. On the hand below, you—as South—could bid your club suit, but by saying Double, you are telling your partner that you have both the remaining suits and you want him to pick the one he prefers:

N	E	S	W
–	–	–	1D
NB	1S	Dbl	

♠ 53
♥ AQJ8
♦ 95
♣ AK742

In this way, you have brought both suits into the picture, shown your shortage in the opponents' suits and opening hand values.

You must be alert when playing Doubles, however. For example, what would you—as South—do here?

N	E	S	W
–	–	–	1D
Dbl	NB	?	

♠ J642
♥ 953
♦ 8642
♣ 76

What a revolting pile of rubbish…Surely, there is nothing to be said here? But this is the key:

When your partner makes a Take-out Double and the next opponent says "No-bid," you MUST bid something. This is because if you said "No-bid" here, your opponent would probably pass as well and the final contract would be 1 Diamond doubled. In itself, that is not a problem. If West makes 1 Diamond doubled, he gets 40 below the line (20 doubled) and a small bonus above the line for making a doubled contract. The problems start when he makes overtricks. Making doubled overtricks is a very lucrative business and can add up to hundreds or even thousands of points in bonuses above the line. You may lose so much in fact that even if your side went on to win the rubber, you would still not win back all the points you lost on this one hand. Hence the rule (repeated because it is so vital):

When your partner makes a Take-out Double and the next opponent says "No-bid," you MUST bid something.

In this example, you will bid 1 Spade (choosing the longer suit of the three unbid suits). Your partner will not get overexcited, because when you bid a suit at the lowest available level it promises no points at all—he knows that you have had to bid something!

If, on the other hand, your right hand opponent bids after your partner has said "Double," then the Double is cancelled and you no longer have to make a bid if you don't want to.

On the occasions when you do have a few points in your hand and your partner doubles for Take-out, it is important that you show him that you have a good hand by jumping in your best suit. Indeed, as responder to a Take-out Double, it is your responsibility to bid as many of your best suit as you think your side can make.

The way I recommend you think is this. When your partner doubles, imagine he holds 13pts and his hand is shaped 4–4–4–1 (with the shortage in the opponents' suit, of course). He may have this hand, or one slightly weaker or a lot stronger, but it gives you an average kind of hand to imagine and makes responding much more straightforward than having to remember rules or point-counts. Then, bid as many of your longest suit as you think your side can make.

Let's look at these examples, in which you are South as usual and your opponent has opened 1 Diamond, your partner has doubled (showing the other three suits and an opening hand, with a shortage in diamonds) and your right hand opponent has passed. What are you going to bid (and remember, because your RHO passed, you MUST bid something)?

N	E	S	W
			1D
Dbl	NB	?	

a) ♠ AQ963   b) ♠ AQ643   c) ♠ AQ862
      ♥ K95   ♥ KJ8   ♥ Q75
      ♦ 872   ♦ 732   ♦ 853
      ♣ A8   ♣ 43   ♣ 54

On all these hands, you are quite happy to bid. Your side is marked with the majority of points and, with five spades, you know that you have at least an 8-card fit in spades, maybe a 9-card fit.

a)   **4 Spades.** Your partner has promised you an opening hand and you have one also. An opening hand opposite an opening hand equals game. You have a definite fit in spades—because the Double guarantees at least 3-card support for every unbid suit—often 4-card support. So, bid as many of your best suit as you think your side can make.

b) **3 Spades.** You have a little less than an opening hand, so you cannot be certain that game is on. Bid 3 Spades here, and if your partner has more than the 13pts you have assumed that he holds, he will bid on to game.

c) **2 Spades.** You still need to jump a level here because, if you bid just 1 Spade, you would be promising no points whatsoever. Here, you have 8pts and a nice 5-card suit, so jump one level to show a decent, if unremarkable, hand. If the doubler is much stronger than the 13pts you assume that he holds, he will bid on. If not, he will pass and you make a safe part-score.

Even if you had held only a 4-card spade suit, you would have made the same bid on each occasion. There is a slight danger that partner may hold only 3-card spade support, but a 7-card fit is not a disaster (we prefer an 8-card fit) and our options are limited anyway, because we are in a competitive auction.

There are further, more complicated responses that you can give to a Take-out Double, but for now these will get you to the right contract 90 percent of the time.

One of the most commonly asked questions in bridge is this: How do I know whether my partner's Double is asking me to bid, or trying to penalize the opponents?

First, let me tell you that this is a question that bothers even the world's best players at times. Double is a very flexible bid and as you improve you will use it more and more often. The good news is that at student and social level, there is a really simple answer to this question and it is this:

- If you have not made a positive bid (whether you haven't had a chance to bid yet or you have said "No-bid"), if your partner doubles then he is asking you to bid.

- If you have made a positive bid, then Double from your partner can't be asking you to bid your best suit—because you've already done that, so it is saying that he wants to penalize your opponents.

For example:

Your partner opens the bidding with 1 Spade, your right hand opponent (RHO) overcalls 2 Hearts and you, as South, hold this hand:

N	E	S	W
1S	2H	?	

♠ 5
♥ KJ743
♦ AK72
♣ 852

You hate your partner's suit and you love your opponent's suit. Can East possibly make eight tricks when your side holds the majority of points and you are sitting over your opponent (that is to say, you are next to play each time your opponent plays a card) with five of his trumps? No! Not in a million years! Even my cat could stop the opponents making eight tricks here...East will have a truly horrible time trying to play in 2 Hearts doubled and your side will get rich (to see penalty scoring, see page 155). Double by you is now for penalties and your partner will know this because he has already made a positive bid.

BRIEFING

Key Elements: Take-Out Double and Responses

1. You can only double an opponent's bid, not your partner's bid.

2. A Double is for penalties if your partner has already made a positive bid; for Take-out, instructing your partner to bid his best unbid suit, if your partner has not yet made a positive bid.

    If your opponents bid uninterrupted to a game contract and suddenly you double, that will also be for penalties because, if you had wanted your partner to bid, you would have doubled earlier in the auction.

3. A Take-out Double shows opening hand values—12pts or more—with a guarantee of 3-card support for every unbid suit—usually 4-card support.

    If your opponents have bid two suits and your partner doubles, he is promising at least 4-card support for both unbid suits. He will usually be 5–4 or 5–5 in the unbid suits.

4. When responding to a Take-out Double, imagine your partner holds a 4–4–4–1 shaped hand with about 13pts, then bid as many of your side's best suit as you think you can make. Don't be shy—bid the maximum you think you can make.

5. If your partner doubles and the next opponent passes, you have to bid however weak you are. When your partner hears you bidding at the lowest available level, he will know that you may hold as few as 0pts.

Overcalls

An overcall is any bid of a suit (or no-trumps) after your opponents have bid. In simple terms, you are "calling over" your opponents' bid.

Whereas Double is a serious competitive bid which often results in your side winning the contract, overcalls and the responses to overcalls are designed with one prime purpose: to disrupt the opponents' bidding sequence.

Sometimes you will steal the contract; sometimes you will find that your side holds the majority of points. But mostly, your desire is to cause trouble by using up the opponents' bidding space and bullying them to beyond a safe level or getting them into the wrong suit as trumps.

You must do all this without risking your opponents making a Penalty Double (see page 74) of your contract. So, you have to combine courage and determination with safe, sensible competition.

The single most important element of an overcall is this:

All overcalls guarantee a 5-card suit or longer.

No exceptions...Ever.

There are several types of overcall, but we will look at just two for now, together with their responses.

Simple Overcalls

A simple overcall is where you bid your suit at the lowest available level over your opponent's opening bid.

If you can bid your suit at the 1-level, you require as few as 8pts and your decent-quality 5-card suit. What is decent quality? At least two of the top four cards will do—although as you become more experienced, you will learn when to stretch these rules...

The point range is very wide—anything from 8pts up to about 17pts...but usually you will have between 8pts and 12pts.

If you have to bid at the 2-level to show your suit, then you require an opening hand (12pts or more) and a 5-card suit (if you have a 6-card suit, perhaps 11pts).

Again, the point range is wide: 11–17pts, but usually you will hold 12 or 13pts.

The reason that you require a much stronger hand to bid at the 2-level than at the 1-level is that a 2-level overcall is promising to make eight tricks if left to play, and it also offers your opponents a chance to double you for penalties if the next opponent holds good cards in your suit (see page 74).

In these examples, your RHO has opened 1 Diamond. Are you going to bid on these hands?

a) ♠ AK86 b) ♠ KQJ96 c) ♠ 86
   ♥ 52   ♥ 853   ♥ AK7
   ♦ J964   ♦ 82   ♦ 32
   ♣ AJ7   ♣ K75   ♣ AQJ864

a) No-bid. You cannot bid on this hand. Despite holding opening hand values, you have no 5-card suit with which to overcall, and you are not suitable for a Take-out Double (see page 75). No-bid is the hardest competitive bid to make in bridge, but it is often right if you do not have a distributional hand.

b) 1 Spade. A perfect 1-level overcall, showing 8pts or more and a decent quality 5-card suit.

c) 2 Clubs. A perfect 2-level overcall. You hold a high-quality 6-card suit and opening hand values.

Responding to Simple Overcalls

Here comes the good part! An overcall can be obstructive on its own but it is far more effective if your partner holds some support and can raise your overcall to a higher level.

This uses up vital bidding space your opponents would far rather preserve.

First, three important thoughts regarding competitive bidding:

1. If your opponents have an 8-card fit in a suit, then your side will almost always have an 8-card fit in one of the other suits. So it is an extra good time to compete when your opponents have found a fit.
2. When your side holds the majority of the points, you try to reach the best contract for your side, using as much bidding as you require to ascertain level and which suit will be trumps.
3. When your side holds the minority of points, your aim is to cause as much disruption as possible to your opponents' bidding, possibly stealing the contract from them at low levels.

So, when you come to responding to your partner's overcall, it will not be the number of points that you hold that will be vital, it will be the number of cards in your partner's suit.

Assuming decent quality trump support, you are safe to raise your partner's overcalled suit to as many tricks as you hold trumps between you. That is to say, if your partner overcalls (promising a 5-card suit) and you hold decent 4-card support, you will usually be safe to bid nine tricks' worth—the 3-level.

You do not expect to make this contract, but you do expect not to fail by more than one or two tricks. Either this will prove cheaper than letting your opponents make their contract or your opponents will continue bidding and perhaps misjudge their correct contract. It is here that we are introducing a vital new principle to our bidding:

It is quite acceptable—indeed, desirable—to fail by one or two tricks in your contract if you are stopping your opponents from making their contract.

This feels quite odd sometimes, but it is a big winning strategy as you will see in the Scoring section on page 153.

So, points are irrelevant when your side holds the minority of points; the number of cards you hold in your longest suit is the key to how high you are prepared to risk competing.

Your LHO opens 1 Diamond; your partner overcalls 1 Spade; your RHO bids 2 Clubs. What, if anything will you—as South—bid on these hands?

N	E	S	W
–	–	–	1D
1S	2C	?	

a)
♠ K86
♥ 9753
♦ J9
♣ K983

b)
♠ AJ96
♥ 4
♦ 8732
♣ KJ92

c)
♠ Q8
♥ KJ75
♦ KJ97
♣ Q95

a) **2 Spades.** You have 3-card support for your partner's overcall, giving you a total of eight cards in spades. You are therefore safe to bid eight tricks' worth. Your side may have as few as 15pts between you (8pts minimum for your partner's 1-level overcall, plus 7pts in your hand), so you probably will not make 2 Spades. However, if you do only have 15pts, your opponents hold 25pts—enough for a possible game contract. If they do bid on, notice that by competing to 2 Spades, your opponents will now have to continue bidding at the 3-level, and this leaves them very little space to investigate their best contract. Hence, you have been very disruptive to them—just how you like it!

b) **3 Spades.** You have nine spades between you, so bid at the nine trick level. Notice that, despite your weak hand, your spades are quite good, and you have a nice singleton in hearts, which means that you can trump your opponents' hearts after the first round.

c) **No-bid.** You cannot raise your partner's suit, as you only hold 2-card support. Despite your good hand, do not bid anything.

The basic rule about responding to overcalls is unbelievably simple, yet it seems to be ignored by players of all standards.

When Responding to an Overcall: Support or Shut Up!

In other words, however good your hand, don't bid anything at all if you cannot raise your partner's suit. Very rarely, you may decide to show a 5- or 6-card major suit of your own—but this happens so infrequently, we won't bother with it now.

Let's look at responding to a 2-level overcall:

N	E	S	W
–	–	–	1S
2D	NB	?	

d)   ♠ 86
     ♥ 97
     ♦ QJ95
     ♣ AJ743

e)   ♠ J962
     ♥ 74
     ♦ KJ6
     ♣ KJ92

f)   ♠ AQ5
     ♥ K5
     ♦ K97
     ♣ J9852

d)   **3 Diamonds.** You have nine diamonds between you, so bid at the nine trick level. This is an effective barrage. If you just pass, your opponents may come back into the auction and discover that they hold a fit in hearts. This way, the opener will have to bid at the 3-level to reenter the auction, and without any support from his partner, he is unlikely to risk that.

e)   **No-bid.** This is a nice hand with good support for your partner. However, you only know that you hold eight diamonds between you so you should not bid any higher than the 2-level. Also, as your partner holds an opening hand and you hold 9pts, you may well find that the opponents stop bidding now, since they probably hold the minority of points.

f)   **3NT.** Oh wow—what's this? Well, think about what your partner has shown you and what you have and put the two together: you have an opening hand and so—to overcall at the 2-level—does your partner. An opening hand opposite an opening hand equals game. You have nice support for partner's 5-card suit, but you do not want to play in 5 Diamonds. Whenever you have a fit in a minor suit, your first thought should be to play in 3NT. Here, you hold good cards in the suit your opponent bid—spades—so he can't run rampant there. You also have decent cards in the unbid suits, so 3NT looks perfect.

Finally, we need to look at a comparatively rare, but vital situation:

N	E	S	W
–	–	–	1D
1S	NB	?	

g)　　♠ K73
　　　♥ A642
　　　♦ A432
　　　♣ K5

You hold an opening hand with support for your partner's overcall. You cannot simply bid 2 Spades, because that would be a weak bid, attempting to barrage your opponents. Bidding 3 Spades or 4 Spades would also be weak, but show longer trump support. This is because all raises of partner's overcall show weak hands (3–11pts). Here, you need to make a bid that says to partner—"I have support for you, but also, we hold the majority of points, so I want to judge what the best contract will be."

With your 14pts, if your partner holds a minimum overcall of 8pts, then 2 Spades will probably be the right contract. If he holds, say 12pts, then you will want to be in game in 4 Spades. How can we wake partner up to ask him to describe his hand further to us?

We need a bid that will really make him jump, so that he realizes that it is his side that holds the majority of points and you are trying to get more information from him.

We will get his attention by making an extraordinary bid. (It has an extraordinary name too "an unassuming cue-bid," but I wouldn't worry about that if I were you.)

We are going to bid our opponents' suit!

So, on this auction (here is the hand and bidding again). We are going to bid 2 Diamonds!

N	E	S	W
–	–	–	1D
1S	NB	?	

g) ♠ K73
    ♥ A642
    ♦ A432
    ♣ K5

This says: "Partner, I guarantee 3-card support for you and an opening hand (12pts or more). If you are minimum for your overcall (about 8pts) then simply rebid your suit at the lowest available level: 2 Spades."

If, on the other hand, you are stronger than you have promised, say 12pts or more, then describe another feature of your hand:

• With a 6-card suit, jump in your suit.
• With another unbid 4-card suit, bid this now.
• With good cards in the opponents' suit, bid no-trumps.

On this occasion, if partner simply rebids 2 Spades to show a minimum hand, you would pass and 2 Spades would be a fine part-score contract. If partner makes any other bid—showing extra points, you could then jump to 4 Spades immediately, because game should be on for your side.

Of course, your partner is not allowed to pass when you bid the opponent's suit; it is a forcing bid. If your partner does pass by mistake, I recommend a good sharp kick under the table. If he does it again, find yourself another partner. We use this bid of the opponent's suit precisely because it is so unusual and it should therefore wake your partner up to what is happening.

Overcalling 1NT

This is the one other type of overcall we will examine here. This bid does not occur very often and the point of this section is rather to stop you making bad bids than to teach you a frequently occurring good bid. Let me show you what I mean:

Your RHO opens 1 Heart, and this is your hand. What do you bid?

N	E	S	W
–	1H	?	

a) ♠ K86   b) ♠ A6   c) ♠ AQ8
   ♥ AQ53   ♥ 942   ♥ KJ75
   ♦ J94   ♦ K8732   ♦ AJ9
   ♣ K93   ♣ KJ9   ♣ Q95

a) **No-bid.** When you have your opponent's suit, you never bid without a massively strong hand (16pts or more). Just pass and hope that they bid hearts at a higher level. Then, you can defeat them.

Although you would have opened 1NT with this hand, you cannot overcall 1NT without more points. Whenever you plan to open 1NT and an opponent opens ahead of you, you must almost always pass.

b) **No-bid.** Your diamond suit is of poor quality and you

are not strong enough to overcall at the 2-level (see page 83). Therefore, you must pass and await developments.

c) **1NT.** To make an overcall of 1NT you require 16–18pts, a reasonably balanced hand, and good cards in your opponent's suit. These good cards are often called "stops" or "stoppers." To overcall 1NT, you will usually require two stoppers—cards to stop the opponent from cashing lots of winners—in the opener's suit.

There is one other type of hand on which you might overcall 1NT and that is a hand containing a long minor suit. You'll be familiar by now with the clarion call: with a minor suit, always support no-trumps.

N	E	S	W
–	1H	?	

d) ♠ J74
♥ AQ
♦ Q4
♣ AQJ732

d) **1NT.** Although this seems a little odd, you don't want to play in 5 Clubs so, if there is game available for your side, it will be in 3NT. Your cards in diamonds and spades are not great but hopefully you will be able to make lots of tricks in clubs before your opponents know what has hit them. Notice that you still hold very good stoppers in the opponent's heart suit to stop them from running away with lots of tricks in that suit.

Responding to a 1NT Overcall

Responding to a 1NT overcall is almost exactly the same as responding to an opening bid of 1NT (page 54), except that the overcall is promising 16–18pts and the opening bid of 1NT only 12–14pts. Therefore, every point-count should be reduced by 4pts to ensure that you reach the right level.

These are the responses to a 1NT overcall:

0–7pts   Pass with a balanced hand; make a Weak Take-out with a 5-card suit or longer.

8–9pts   Invite game with a raise to 2NT with a balanced hand or one containing a long minor suit; bid a 5-card major suit at the 3-level or 6-card major suit at the game level.

10pts+   Raise to 3NT with a balanced hand or one containing a long minor suit; bid a 5-card major suit at the 3-level or 6-card major suit at the game level.

Making and Responding to Overcalls

Suit Overcalls

1. All overcalls guarantee a decent quality 5-card suit or longer. Their prime objective is to obstruct your opponents' auction.

2. 1-level overcalls may be as weak as 8pts, and as strong as 17pts, but the usual range is about 8–12pts.

    2-level overcalls must show an opening hand or better (or perhaps 11pts with a 6-card suit). The usual range is 12–14pts.

3. Responding to overcalls: if you do not have support for partner's suit, just pass—"Support or shut up!"

4. If you have a weak hand, say 3–11pts, support your partner's suit as a barrage. You are safe to bid as many tricks as you have cards in your long suit, provided that you have at least one high card in your partner's suit.

    If you have a strong hand with at least 3-card support for partner's suit, make an "unassuming cue-bid"—bidding the opener's suit at the lowest available level.

    If your partner is minimum for his overcall, he rebids his suit at the lowest level; if he is stronger he describes his hand further.

1NT Overcall

1. A 1NT overcall shows 16–18pts, with good cards (stoppers) in the opponent's suit.

2. A 1NT overcall may not be a completely balanced hand if it contains a long minor suit.

3. When responding to a 1NT overcall, think of your responses to an opening 1NT bid—and remember that you will need 4pts less for each response as the 1NT overcall has promised 4pts more than a 1NT opener.

12

Conventions: Description of Stayman and Blackwood

Up until now, all our bidding has been what we call "natural." That is to say, when we bid clubs it is because we have a club suit; when we bid no-trumps, we have a balanced hand, and so on.

Top players soon realized, however, that there were many bids that players would very rarely or never make. These were therefore wasted bids in a language that was pretty restricted already, so they invented new "conventional" or artificial meanings for these bids.

There are many different conventions: some good, some bad, but the two included here are so widely played that all half-decent bridge players learn and play them. Indeed, it would be surprising these days to find a social or club bridge player who doesn't play both these conventions.

Because these conventions are quite advanced, we won't look at them in detail now, but instead just take a look at what they do and their basic mechanisms. Then when your friends ask you if you know "Stayman" and "Blackwood" you can tell them that you know what they are about, but that you haven't learned them fully yet—I think they'll be impressed.

Stayman

This convention was promoted by Mr. Sam Stayman throughout the United States and it soon became very popular. Its purpose is to discover, after partner has opened the bidding with 1NT, whether a 4–4 fit in a major suit exists. You use it only after an opening bid of 1NT (and sometimes after an overcall of 1NT as well) to find out whether the 1NT opener's hand contains four hearts or four spades. This is how it operates (but remember, this is a quick outline only, not the full works):

In response to your partner's 1NT opener, on suitable hands you make a bid of 2 Clubs. Once you have agreed to play the Stayman convention, your 2 Clubs no longer means a Weak Take-out into clubs (see page 54), but instead begins this artificial convention.

It says to your partner that you have sufficient points to cope with all his responses (usually 11pts or more) and that your hand definitely contains four hearts or four spades or both. You are then asking him whether he has four hearts or four spades in his hand.

If the 1NT opener's hand contains a 4-card spade suit, he responds 2 Spades.

If it contains a 4-card heart suit, he responds 2 Hearts.

If it contains neither four hearts nor four spades, he responds 2 Diamonds.

This last response is again an artificial bid, not saying anything about diamonds, but just acting as a negative response to partner's question.

you	partner
♠ KJ	♠ A42
♥ AQ86	♥ K973
♦ K743	♦ AJ85
♣ 973	♣ J2
—	1NT
2C	2H
4H	

Your partner deals and opens the bidding with 1NT. Your opponents pass throughout. You are about to raise your partner to 3NT, when you consider that you might have a 4–4 fit in hearts. Remembering that a 4–4 fit in a major suit is top of your order of priorities (see page 50), you use Stayman to discover whether your partner holds a 4-card major within his 1NT bid. When partner responds 2 Hearts, showing a 4-card heart suit, you now know that you have your major suit fit. Since you have an opening hand opposite your partner's opening hand, you don't waste a moment—and you bid 4 Hearts immediately.

If your partner gives you the response you did not wish to hear, you bid whatever you would have bid anyway, as if you had never bothered with Stayman in the first place.

you	partner
♠ A987	♠ 62
♥ J8	♥ KQ73
♦ K97	♦ AQ85
♣ QJ98	♣ K72

—	1NT
2C	2H
2NT	3NT

Here, your partner deals and opens the bidding with 1NT. Your opponents pass throughout. You are about to raise your partner to 2NT—showing 11–12pts and a balanced hand, when you realize that you may have a 4–4 spade fit, so you try a Stayman bid of 2 Clubs. Your partner shows you a 4-card heart suit and, as that is not what you wanted to hear, you go back to your original plan and bid 2NT. Your partner, with a maximum hand, raises to 3NT.

Notice that you do not need to bid your spade suit. Firstly, you are not allowed to bid a suit after a 1NT opening without five cards. Secondly, your partner knows that you have a 4-card spade suit. Why? Because, when you used Stayman, you were promising that you held at least one 4-card major suit. When your partner showed four hearts and you failed to support him, he will know that you must have four spades instead. Should he have both majors, he can support your spades next time around.

To make a Weak Take-out (with 0–10pts) and a 6-card club suit or longer, bid 2 Clubs (which everyone will take as Stayman) and then rebid 3 Clubs over whatever response your partner gives you. This cancels Stayman and shows a Weak Take-out hand in clubs, which your partner will pass.

So, there is an outline of Stayman. It needs more study and further detail before you can play it confidently, but you know now what it is, why you make the bid, and basically how it works.

Blackwood

Mr. Easeley Blackwood gave his name to this convention, which is a slam-going conventional bid. We have not talked much about slams because they very rarely occur. However, since this convention is played throughout the world, it is at least worth knowing what it is all about.

There are several different versions of Blackwood, but we will look at the standard version on which all the clever-clever variations are based. When you come to learn this, or one of the variations, I think you will find it easy to grasp.

The bid that starts this convention is 4NT. The reason why this bid is used is because it has no other practical purpose. Why bid 4NT when 3NT gives you a game contract? Nobody would ever bid 4NT for the fun of it, so it is a spare bid that can be used when considering a slam.

To bid a slam, you need lots of points between you and your partner, a good robust trump suit (or good cards in each suit for a no-trump contract) and aces. Without aces, you will lose tricks very quickly. So, to be in a slam you need to hold at least three—preferably all four—aces between you and your partner. The Blackwood convention is used to ask your partner how many aces he holds in his hand.

Use Blackwood only when you are virtually certain that you want to bid a slam. Use it only when you know which suit will be trumps (or no-trumps), and check that you can cope with any of the responses your partner may give you. If your agreed suit is clubs, for example, partner's response may take you past the 5 Club level and commit you to a slam. Check that you think your bid is worth the risk.

A bid of 4NT asks partner how many aces he holds in his hand.

All the responses are conventional (or artificial) and they follow the order of suits that you learned right at the beginning (page 6).

5C	says that you hold no aces in your hand.
5D	says that you hold one ace.
5H	says that you hold two aces.
5S	says that you hold three aces.

Should you happen to hold all four aces when your partner asks you—which is very unlikely—then the response for all four aces is 5 Clubs.

I know that this is the same as no aces, but it really is impossible to confuse no aces with four aces. From the bidding up to this point you will be able to tell the difference—it is 16pts worth after all.

If you have all four aces between you and you think you might be able to make a Grand Slam (a 7-level contract) then you can ask your partner for kings with a bid of 5NT. This is very rare.

Again, the responses follow the order of suits:

6C	says no kings.
6D	shows one king.
6H	shows two kings.
6S	shows three kings.
6NT	shows all four kings.

Once the player who has started Blackwood by bidding 4NT has heard all he needs to hear, he decides what the final contract should be and partner leaves it at that.

Stayman and Blackwood

Stayman operates only in response to an opening bid of 1NT and is designed to locate a 4–4 fit in a major suit.

Playing Stayman, a response of 2 Clubs is no longer a Weak Take-out, but shows that your hand contains a 4-card major suit and asks whether the 1NT opener's hand contains a 4-card major suit as well. In reply:

2D   shows no 4-card major suit.

2H   shows four hearts (and maybe even four spades because if you hold four hearts and four spades you should bid hearts first).

2S   shows four spades.

The Stayman bidder passes or raises the major suit if he finds a 4–4 fit.

With no fit, the Stayman bidder says whatever he would have bid without using Stayman—usually 2NT or 3NT.

Usually—not always—but usually, you will require 11pts to use Stayman.

To make a Weak Take-out (with 0–10pts) and a 6-card club suit or longer, bid 2 Clubs (which everyone will take as Stayman) and then rebid 3 Clubs over whatever response your partner gives you. This cancels Stayman and shows a Weak Take-out hand in clubs, which your partner will pass.

Blackwood is a convention used to ask partner how many aces (and sometimes kings) his hand contains on the way to bidding a slam.

You must know that your side contains sufficient points and which suit will be trumps before using Blackwood. Bid 4NT.

In reply:

5C   shows no or four aces.
5D   shows one ace.
5H   shows two aces.
5S   shows three aces.

Only if your partnership holds all four aces between you and your target is a Grand Slam should you ask for kings. Bid 5NT. In reply:

6C   shows no kings.
6D   shows one king.
6H   shows two kings.
6S   shows three kings.
6NT   shows four kings.

PART THREE

The Play of the Cards

13
No-Trump Contracts

No-trump contracts strike fear into even the brave. This is because there is usually a right way and a wrong way to play each hand, and once you are on the wrong track, your opponents can rattle off tricks galore in a suit and you can do nothing to stop them. For this reason, keeping control is a vital factor of play in no-trumps.

Let's look immediately at an example. As in the rest of this book, you will be the South hand, and your partner will be North and dummy.

N	E	S	W
–	–	1NT	NB
3NT			

♠ KQ7
♥ A64
♦ K753
♣ Q85

West's opening lead: 3♥

	N	
W		E
	S	

♠ J1098
♥ KJ8
♦ A2
♣ A742

You and your partner (South and North) reach 3NT easily and West leads 3♥. It is West who leads because you, as South, were the first player to mention no-trumps, which becomes the final denomination in which your side is playing. We will look at leads later on (page 128), but against no-trump contracts, opponents usually lead a low card in their longest suit, provided that it has not been bid by you and your partner. Dummy now gets laid down on the table.

Now, wait—do not touch a card from dummy yet. This is a vital moment and you must take your time. Have a good look at dummy and see how it fits with your own hand. Then go through each of the suits, working out how many tricks you could win immediately. These are called top tricks. Let's do that now.

In spades: You have no top tricks because you are missing A♠.

In hearts: You have three top tricks: A♥, K♥, and also J♥ because the lead is coming around the table and ending up in your hand: if you

play low from dummy—as you should—
and, if East plays low, you can win with J♥;
if East plays Q♥, you can win with K♥ and
your J♥ is good.

In diamonds: You have two top tricks: A♦ and K♦.

In clubs: You have one top trick: A♣.

So, you have six top tricks and you need three more. These
will usually come from the suit in which you have most
cards between your two hands. Here, it is the spade suit
that offers extra tricks, as once A♠ is pushed out from your
opponent's hand, you will have three winners in the suit.

The key is to keep control. If you win the first trick and
then play out all your winners, you will have six tricks in
front of you. However, when you play on spades, your opponents will gain the lead with A♠ and they will have winning cards in the other suits because you have played out
the aces and kings, and you will not be able to stop them.
So, this is always your basic plan in no-trumps:

**Push out (by playing the suit until your oppo-
nents win the trick with their high card in that suit)
the cards you have to lose before enjoying any of
your winners.**

Let's play the hand together. You play a low heart from
dummy and East plays 9♥, allowing you to win with your
J♥. Do not play out any other winners! Instead, aim to
push out A♠ while you still have stoppers (cards which will
stop the opponents from winning tricks) in each suit. Play
on spades immediately. Continue playing on spades until
the opponent with A♠ plays it. Whatever he leads next, you
will be able to win, and now, you have nine tricks: three
spades, three hearts, two diamonds, and one club.

When you have enough tricks to make your contract—
and not until—you can play them out.

You made your 3NT contract by keeping control of each suit.

Let's take a look at another way of keeping control on a different deal with all four hands shown. Try not to look at the East-West cards because taking in all fifty-two cards is a tall order. Just look at the North-South cards again.

N	E	S	W
–	–	1NT	NB
3NT			

♠ Q73
♥ 85
♦ A32
♣ KQJ85

♠ J84		♠ 10952
♥ KQJ94	N	♥ 1072
♦ Q106	W E	♦ J74
♣ 96	S	♣ A103

♠ AK6
♥ A63
♦ K985

West's opening lead: K♥   ♣ 742

You find yourself again in 3NT. West leads K♥—which is the top of a sequence of honor cards (see page 129).

The first thing you do is pause, look at dummy and your own hand, and count your top tricks. Here we go:

In spades	Three top tricks: ♠AKQ.
In hearts	One top trick: the ace.
In diamonds	Two top tricks: A♦ and K♦.
In clubs	No top tricks as you are missing the ace.

So, you have six top tricks and you require three more. They will come from your longest suit, clubs. Before you can make any tricks, however, you have to push out A♣. Can you see any problems?

The heart suit is your problem here because you only have one stopper—the ace—between your two hands. Once this is gone, you will be exposed in hearts and East-West can cash winners there and defeat you. Watch what happens:

If you win the first trick with A♥ and then play on clubs, East will win his A♣ immediately and he will lead back a heart to his partner. With no high cards left in hearts to stop him, West will reel off four more winners which, when added to East's A♣, is five tricks—and that is one too many for you.

To try to prevent this from happening—and to keep control—you need to adopt a "hold-up" play. This play is designed to exhaust at least one of your opponents of his supply of the suit about which you are worried. In this way, if he gains the lead later on, he will have no cards left in his hand to lead back to his partner. Watch what happens if we adopt the hold-up play here:

You duck (that is to say, you refuse to win) the first round of hearts, allowing West to win his K♥. He will lead Q♥ and this you should also duck. He will then lead J♥ and this time you have no choice but to win with your A♥. Remembering that you cash no other winners until you have pushed out any high cards you need to dislodge in order to set up your extra tricks, you play immediately on clubs, leading a low club from your hand, planning to play dummy's K♣ unless West plays A♣ first. In fact, East holds A♣, so when you play dummy's K♣, East takes the trick with the ace. However, because three rounds of hearts have already been played, he has no hearts left to lead back to his partner! Whatever he now plays, you can win and play out your winners, ending up with ten tricks, provided that you play carefully and accurately. Lay out the hands with real cards in front of you and play it through. You should find that, played correctly, by the end you will make these tricks as follows: three spades, one heart, two diamonds, and four clubs.

So as a general rule, when you have only one stopper (high card) in a suit led by your opponents, refuse to take the trick until the last possible moment. Then, hopefully, one of your opponents will have no cards left in that suit, and when he regains the lead, the communication is cut between your two opponents' hands.

There are many other ways to improve your chances of scoring your contract, which build on these ideas and introduce new ones. One of the most important is "the finesse," which we will examine later.

BRIEFING

No-Trump Play

1. When dummy is put down, do not hurry! Look carefully at your hand and dummy.

2. Count the number of tricks you could take immediately (top tricks). If you have enough to make your contract, cash them out. If you do not have enough tricks to make your contract, do not play out any winners yet!

3. Decide from which suit you will try to make your extra tricks (usually the suit in which you hold most cards between your two hands) and attack that suit while you still have high cards to protect all your other suits. When you can count enough tricks to make your contract, then take them.

4. If your opponents lead a suit in which you hold only one stopper, it is usual to duck this trick for as long as possible, trying to exhaust at least one opponent (usually the partner of the opponent who has led the suit) of his supply of that suit.

5. **Key Thought:**
   To keep control, push out your opponents' high cards before enjoying any of your winning cards in other suits.

14
Suit Contracts

Suit (or Trump) contracts require a different approach from no-trump contracts, offering—as they do—a variety of different possibilities to succeed. Once again, when dummy is first laid down, the declarer should take his time to look at his hand in relation to the dummy and to form a basic plan of attack.

However, instead of counting your top tricks (as in no-trumps) in suit contracts, it is better to assess which cards you are likely to lose, and then set about working on how to avoid losing those tricks. The power of the trump suit becomes apparent very quickly as you look at your two main lines of play. Here is a straightforward example that demonstrates the main possibilities when considering your play.

N	E	S	W
–	–	1H	NB
3H	NB	4H	

♠ QJ
♥ J973
♦ A4
♣ QJ865

West's opening lead: A♠

```
    N
W       E
    S
```

♠ 82
♥ AKQ85
♦ J83
♣ AK2

You reach your game contract of 4 Hearts with ease. West leads A♠ and, before playing from dummy, you assess the situation. Look at each suit and analyze how many losers (cards with which you expect to lose the trick) you have. Do this by concentrating on the shape of your hand, and using dummy's high cards to fill the gaps where you can.

In spades, you have two losers, because you have two little cards in your own hand, and dummy contains ♠QJ. However, as you are missing ♠AK, that will result in the loss of two tricks.

In hearts, you have no losers, because you hold all the top honors between your two hands.

In diamonds, you have two losers because, although dummy contains the ace, you hold two further low cards in your hand.

Finally, in clubs, you have no losers: you hold ♣AK in your hand, and dummy contains Q♣ to cover your 2♣.

You have four losers and that is one too many. How can you get rid of one of your losers?

There are two main ways by which you can dispose of losers. These are described more fully below but, in short, comprise:

1. **Trump losing cards, using dummy's trumps.** As you are counting losers in your own hand, trumping with your own trumps does not help you. But, trumping with dummy's trumps means that you are making extra tricks.

2. **Throw away losing cards on dummy's long suit.** If dummy has a suit that contains more cards than the holding in your own hand, it is considered to be a long suit. Use this to discard your losing cards in other suits from hand.

There are variations and additional advanced plays that can add to your chances of success, but remarkably, these two rules will cover over 95 percent of the hands you play.

Let's see what we could do on the hand above.

Here, you are in the luxurious position of being able to choose between both possible lines of play.

Trumping in dummy. You could, at a later stage in the hand, win the trick with A♦, then play a little diamond and lose it to your opponents. Now, there will be a void (no cards) in diamonds left in the dummy hand, and when you regain the lead, you can play your third diamond from your hand and trump it with one of dummy's trumps.

Using dummy's long suit. Alternatively, you could play out the trump suit until your opponents have no trumps left in their hand, and then play A♣, K♣, and your 2♣ over to dummy's Q♣. You can now play dummy's J♣

and throw away one diamond loser. Dummy's 8♣, which by now will almost certainly be the only club left, can be played and you can throw away your second low diamond.

Drawing Trumps

The trump suit is your own, chosen master suit for this hand and you would prefer your opponents not to have any of that suit in their hands. This is why you will often opt to draw out the trumps from your opponents' hands. The best way to keep track of the trump suit is to work out at the start of the hand how many trumps your opponents hold between them, and then to deduct one from that total every time you see them produce a trump card. In this way, you do not have to remember whether you used trumps or how many you started with—merely watch each trump as it appears from your opponents.

When you have few enough losers to claim your contract—whether that is at the start of the hand or after you have undertaken a play to reduce your losers—draw trumps immediately. This way, you will stop your opponents from leaping in and surprising you by trumping your trick.

However, when you have too many losers to make your contract, hesitate before drawing out the trumps. You may need the trumps in dummy to trump losers from your own hand, or you may need dummy's trumps to use as entries (means of access) to get into the dummy hand. Often, you will have to start your line of attack to rid yourself of extra losers while trumps still remain in your opponents' hands. Judgment about when it is right to draw trumps takes time to learn—and, sadly, experience is the best tutor here.

Let's look at two precise examples outlining play techniques:

N	E	S	W
–	–	1S	NB
2S	NB	3S	

♠ KQ2
♥ J
♦ 97532
♣ 8653

West's opening lead: K♥

♠ AJ985
♥ A76
♦ AK
♣ J42

South has been a little frisky pushing on to 3 Spades after North's weak raise, but the contract is a good one. West leads K♥, and before touching dummy, declarer counts his losers—remembering to look at the shape of his own hand, and the high cards which can help in dummy.

No spade losers	–	You hold all the top ones between you.
Two heart losers	–	South's ♥76 will lose tricks.
No diamond losers	–	With ♦AK alone, you can trump any other diamonds that are led.
Three club losers	–	North-South are missing ♣AKQ.

So, South has five losers and can only afford four losers. Can he set up a long suit in dummy, or can he trump losers using dummy's trumps?

The correct line is to use dummy's singleton heart to make at least one heart ruff in dummy. South wins West's

K♥ lead with his A♥. He does not draw trumps, because he needs dummy's trumps to deal with his heart losers. He immediately plays 6♥ from his hand and trumps it with dummy's 2♠. He can now return to hand (i.e. bring the lead back to his own hand) using his A♦ and play his 7♥, this time trumping with dummy's Q♠. Now, with the two heart losers dealt with, South has few enough losers to make his contract, so he draws trumps immediately. He plays K♠ from dummy—noting when each opponent follows suit, and then returns to hand with K♦. Now, he plays his A♠ and his J♠. Hopefully, by then, neither opponent will hold any more spades. If that is so, South will make his 3-Spade contract with an overtrick. Of his five losers, three club tricks must still be lost, but both his two heart losers were trumped in dummy and no longer lost tricks.

N	E	S	W
–	–	1S	NB
2C	NB	2S	NB
3S	NB	4S	

♠ KJ7
♥ 64
♦ 984
♣ AK653

♠ 86   ♠ 93
♥ AK1083   ♥ 952
♦ A105   ♦ QJ632
♣ 974   ♣ Q108

♠ AQ10542
♥ QJ7
♦ K7
West's opening lead: A♥   ♣ J2

Again, North-South have been aggressive in bidding all the way to game, and this time, there seems no way to avoid losing four tricks. But, let's see:

No losers in spades   –   North-South hold all the top cards.

Two losers in hearts   –   North-South are missing ♥AK.

Two losers in diamonds–   If K♦ loses to A♦, his 7♦ will also lose.

No losers in clubs   –   ♣AK in dummy covers your two small clubs in your South hand, and you can then trump any further clubs led by your opponents.

So, there are four losers and South can only afford three. He cannot trump any of those losers in dummy, because there are no shortages that can be used for trumping. The only hope lies in "establishing" dummy's long suit to provide a discard for one of those losers. In order to do this, declarer—South—will have to attack clubs straightaway and trump one of dummy's little clubs in his own hand in order to use up the club supply of his opponents. In doing so, the remaining clubs should become "established"—that is to say, set up as winning cards.

Let's see the play in action.

West leads A♥ and follows it with K♥—which, at least, sets up South's Q♥ as a winner. If West made the mistake of bashing out his A♦ now, South would be home and dry as his K♦ would be a winner and not a loser. But, West knows better than that and is saving his A♦ for South's likely K♦. Instead, he plays a trump. South has already noted that the defenders hold four trumps between them, so when he wins this trick with dummy's J♠, he notes that two of those outstanding trumps have appeared, leaving two out. Now South must attack dummy's long suit immediately. He plays dummy's A♣ and K♣ and then he plays a low club and trumps it in his hand—using 10♠ in case West has run out of clubs. Notice that he is not ruffing in his own hand for the fun of it—he is trying to exhaust East-West of their supply of clubs. Indeed, each opponent follows suit to each round, so dummy's two remaining clubs—♣65—are both winners and can be used to discard losers from South's hand. However, trumps must be taken out of the opponents' hands first or they will trump dummy's winning clubs. So, South plays A♠ from his hand—taking out East and West's last trumps—and then a little spade over to dummy's K♠. South can now play dummy's ♣65 safely and throw away both his diamonds—one of which is the king. All the rest of the cards in his hand are high and winners.

Notice that South did not draw out the trumps until he had established his club suit. He relied on K♠ (and might even have needed 7♠) as an entry to get into the dummy hand.

On every suit contract you play then you must look to make one of two plans:

Ruffing the losers in your hand with dummy's trumps

or

setting up dummy's long suit—perhaps by ruffing low cards in hand—in order to set up winners to throw away your losing cards in hand.

15
Finesses

The finesse is an exciting development for new bridge players because it begins to demonstrate a little bit of bridge magic—producing tricks from nowhere.

If you become a really good player, you will learn that the finesse is quite a blunt instrument in the quest to do away with your opponents, but for now it is the best new weapon we have.

Let's take a look at a finesse, just concentrating on one suit.

Imagine you are South in these examples, and dummy is North.

♠ 743

♠ AQ5

You would like to make two tricks from the spade suit here, but if you play a low card from your hand, either opponent could win with the eight. If you lead the queen from your hand, whichever opponent holds the king will take the trick with it. If you play spades from your own hand, only your A♠ will win a trick.

However, if you lead a little card from the dummy hand, East will have to play before you. If East holds K♠ and plays low, you can "finesse" by playing your Q♠ and that will hold the trick.

Of course, West may have K♠ all along and he will take your Q♠ and you will only make one trick. But, this way, you are giving yourself a 50 percent chance to make an extra trick.

By the way, you may be wondering why East didn't play K♠. If he held it, it would be a foolish thing to do, because it would mean you could win with your A♠ and then play your Q♠ without having to worry...So East will play a little spade from his hand, even if he has the king, because he is hoping you will play your ace anyway. As a general rule, the player who plays the second card to a trick usually plays a low card, allowing his partner—in the last position—to decide whether to win the trick or not.

Let's look at some more examples:

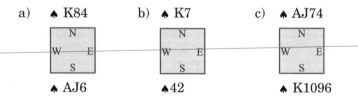

a) ♠ K84   b) ♠ K7   c) ♠ AJ74

♠ AJ6   ♠42   ♠ K1096

a) You have two certain tricks (♠AK) but the only way to make a third trick is to make J♠ count. Lead 4♠ from dummy and, when East plays low, put on J♠ from your hand, hoping that East holds Q♠.

Leading a low card from the North hand makes East—your opponent—play before you have to decide which card to play from your hand. If East plays Q♠, you can beat it with A♠; if East plays low, you finesse with J♠ and hope that West does not produce Q♠.

There is no point leading J♠ from your hand because whoever holds Q♠ will put Q♠ on top of J♠. Even if you then win with K♠, you will have two low cards left in your hands to lose at trick 3.

b) The K♠ will only make a trick if West holds A♠, otherwise East will sit with his ace until you play your king and then he will win. So, you must lead towards K♠. When you play 2♠ from your hand, either West wins with the ace immediately—in which case your king is now a winner—or West plays low and your K♠ holds the trick.

Of course, if East holds A♠, there is nothing you can do.

c) This is an odd one. It is what we call a "two-way finesse" because you can take the finesse in either direction.

If you thought that West held Q♠, you could play a low card from your hand, and when West played small, you could play J♠ from dummy and this would hold the trick…When you cashed ♠AK, the rest of the suit should be winners.

If you thought East held Q♠, you could lead 4♠ from dummy, and, when East played low, you could play 10♠ from your hand and this would hold the trick.

Of course, you have to know which opponent holds
Q♠—or just guess. Those are skills you will learn as
you get better at the game—and, I suspect, more
addicted.

And never lead a high card for a finesse unless you have
the card beneath it—either in your own hand or in dummy.
Let me show you why...

♠ A43

♠ KJ5

You are trying to make three tricks. My cat could make two,
because of ♠AK, but the third one is the tough one. Which
hand do you want Q♠ to be in? East or West?

You want it in the East hand, because if West holds
Q♠, your J♠ will always lose to that card. If you incorrectly
led J♠ from your hand, West would cover that with his Q♠
to push out dummy's A♠. Now, all you have left is K♠ and
two little cards—and your trick total will be just two.

However, if East holds Q♠, you can lead towards the
card you are hoping to win cheaply—the jack. You play 3♠
from dummy, East plays low, and you play J♠. That holds
the trick and you still have ♠AK for two more tricks.

So, when finessing, you only rarely get the chance to
cope with a missing honor in either hand. Usually, you
have to hope it is one hand and if it isn't, you fail.

Finally, let's see why a defender would cover your J♠
with Q♠ if he could...it is known as "covering an honor
with an honor" and, as a very general rule, it is worth
thinking about.

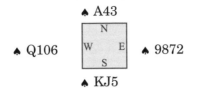

♠ A43

♠ Q106

♠ 9872

♠ KJ5

South incorrectly plays J♠—why should West play Q♠ when he can see that dummy will take it with A♠? He should do so because, if he does not cover J♠, declarer may play low from dummy and win the trick with J♠. More importantly, if West covers the J♠ with Q♠, he is assured a trick, because South must then play A♠ to win the trick and West's 10♠ will automatically win the third round.

Even if West didn't hold 10♠, he should put his honor on top of his opponents' honor to force out A♠ in case his partner holds 10♠.

This is why you must not lead a high card for a finesse, unless you hold the card beneath it. Lead towards the card you want to make a trick with—never lead that card itself!

There are many other elements to finessing and to good defense, and these will be covered in more advanced books, but, once again, follow these outline rules and you will play well most of the time.

16

Defending Your Opponents' Contracts: Basic Strategies and Opening Leads

The defenders are the pair who have to try to stop the opponents from making their contract. Sometimes, the sheer weight of points held by your opponents means that their contract is unbeatable. Sometimes, however, good defense can prevent your opponents from succeeding, and that is what you are always aiming for.

There are two basic strategies for the players who must defend against the contract, depending upon the contracts they are defending: no-trump contracts and suit contracts. Let's look at each in turn.

No-Trump Contracts

Almost all no-trump contracts are a simple race between the declarer and the defense to set up enough tricks for their side either to make their contract or to break it.

For this reason, most defenders will lead their longest suit and continue to play it whenever they gain the lead. In this way, the small cards at the bottom of the suit become winners.

N	E	S	W
–	–	1NT	NB
3NT			

```
                        ♠ K82
                        ♥ AK
                        ♦ 1095
                        ♣ K6543
        ♠ J95         ┌─────┐      ♠ Q1063
        ♥ QJ1086      │  N  │      ♥ 942
        ♦ A84         │W   E│      ♦ 632
        ♣ 97          │  S  │      ♣ A108
                      └─────┘
                        ♠ A74
                        ♥ 753
                        ♦ KQJ7
West's opening lead: Q♥   ♣ QJ2
```

North-South reach 3NT in two easy bids. West, being to the left of the player who first mentioned the denomination (here, no-trumps) in which his side plays, leads his longest suit, knowing that once his opponents' high cards have been dislodged, the length of the suit will produce tricks. This is exactly the same plan as the declarer will have, but the defense have the advantage of leading the first card—so, at this stage, they are ahead in the race.

South wins the first trick with dummy's K♥ and immediately leads a club, planning to push out A♣ as soon as

possible to set up extra tricks. East grabs the trick with his
A♣ immediately and leads back a heart. This may look
odd, with dummy holding the ace, but it is vital!

When East returns his partner's led suit, dummy must
play A♥ and now, if the defense ever gains the lead once
more, the rest of West's hearts will be winners. Sure enough,
South does not have enough tricks to make 3NT and must
hope to score some diamond tricks. So, he plays a diamond,
West leaps in with his A♦ and cashes his three remaining
heart tricks to defeat the contract. No other defense suc-
ceeds: hearts must be led, returned, and then enjoyed, to
beat the contract.

If your partner had bid a suit during the auction, you
would lead his suit, but in general, if your side has not bid
during the auction, the best lead to make against a no-
trump contract is your longest suit, provided it has not already been bid by your opponents. There are other options,
but this will prove best most of the time.

So, which card do you lead?

There are three key elements here, and as you will
practice them every time you play bridge, they will soon
become second nature.

1. Top-of-a-Sequence

Whenever you hold three honor cards (out of ace, king,
queen, jack, or ten) at the head of your suit, you must lead
an honor card. To do so you must hold two cards in a row
because the lead of an honor always promises the card beneath it.

♠ KQJ73   Lead K♠—top of a sequence—you have
                 three honors in a row so, once you have
                 pushed out A♠ the rest of your suit will be

winners. Leading K♠ promises Q♠ and either J♠ or 10♠ or both.

♠ QJ964   Lead Q♠—again top of a sequence—you have two honors in a row and then the next but one.

2. Fourth Highest

If you hold a good quality suit but it is not headed by three honor cards, then you should lead a little card. The lead of a low card indicates that you have good cards at the head of the suit, but that they are not in sequence because if you had held a sequence, you would have led top of a sequence.

You should play the fourth highest card in the suit because, as you become more experienced, that routine will help you and your partner to uncover the distribution of the hand. But that is jumping ahead—let's get you into good habits for now.

♠ K1083   Lead 3♠—you hold two honors at the head of the suit—so lead a little card to indicate interest in the suit.

♠ AJ962   Lead 6♠—a low card indicating interest at the head of the suit.

Both top of a sequence and fourth highest leads suggest that you want your partner to try to win the trick and then, when he regains the lead, you want him to return that suit back to you.

3. High Card from Weakness

If, however, you decide that you have no decent quality suit (that your opponents have not bid during the auction), you may be forced to make a more passive lead from a poorer quality suit. Hence, you want to lead a high intermediate (that is to say, not an honor) card to indicate lack of interest in the suit led. This is often called "top of rubbish."

| ♠ 8752 | Lead 8♠—a high intermediate card indicates a bad quality suit. |
| ♠ 10742 | Lead 7♠—a ten on its own does not count as an honor, so this is considered a bad quality suit. As the ten might be important later, however, save it and lead the second highest card instead. |

When partner sees a high intermediate card (usually 6, 7, 8, or 9) he will deduce that you do not like the suit and that you have no particular desire for your partner to return it to you unless he has some good reason for doing so. Above all, remember that when defending against a no-trump contract, it is the length of the suit that is its strength, and not just the high cards that might take tricks.

The underlying rule here is to attack one suit and to continue attacking it (unless it looks plainly wrong to do so, or you hold a suit so strong that you know it must be right to lead that instead of returning partner's lead) until the declarer loses control of the hand, your side regains the lead, and you are able to cash the winners you have fought to establish.

Suit Contracts

There are more possibilities when defending a suit contract because of the trump situation. You need to be aware of declarer's two likely plans in order to start your defense. Since declarer will aim either to trump losers in dummy or to establish a long suit in dummy, the moment you can see the dummy you will be able to defend more clearly. How-ever, listening to the auction to guess how dummy will look will put you ahead of the game and in with a shout to de-feat your opponent.

Remember that you cannot see the dummy hand until you have made your first lead. If the defender could see dummy before he made his first lead, it would give the de-fenders too much of a chance of beating the contract.

However, if from the bidding you think that the dummy is likely to contain a shortage that the declarer will want to use for ruffs, or if you think your opponents have stretched themselves to bid game, try leading a trump. Don't lead trumps if you hold only a singleton trump (you might spoil what your partner holds that way) or lead a low card from Qxx or Jxxx (where x represents any non-honor card), as this may cost you a trick. However, if you have two, three, or even four low value cards in trumps, you can make a fine lead. If you do lead a trump, always lead your lowest, even if there is a sequence of cards.

If, on the other hand, you think that the dummy will contain a long suit, attack the two suits other than trumps and the long suit in dummy—and attack them aggres-sively. If you don't take your tricks quickly, the declarer will draw trumps and then throw away all his losers from hand using dummy's long suit.

Let me show you what I mean:

N	E	S	W
–	1S	NB	2S
NB	3S	NB	4S

This is not a confident auction. West made a simple raise from 1 Spade to 2 Spades and then East has invited West to bid game by bidding 3 Spades. West has decided that, as he is maximum for his bid, he will give and has given 4 Spades a shot, but the chances are that East-West are short on points. If you are short of points, what is your one chance of making extra tricks? Trumping in one hand or the other, or even both. So, as the defenders, you should attack that extra chance straightaway—by leading trumps. Lead a trump at trick one and continue to lead them every time your side gains the lead. Declarer will almost certainly fail.

N	E	S	W
–	1H	NB	2D
NB	2H	NB	3D
NB	4H		

Here, East-West have had an argument over which suit to have as trumps—diamonds or hearts—but the conclusion is that East holds six or seven high quality hearts and West the same in diamonds. Clubs and spades are unbid and unless you take your tricks quickly in one or both of those suits, the declarer will draw trumps and then play out dummy's long diamond suit throwing away all his spade and club losers. So lead clubs or spades, following the standard rules.

Notice that assessing what dummy will look like is tough, and even then not an exact science, so you may get it wrong. But imagination and deduction are two vital attributes to becoming a good bridge player.

The other factor to remember is that allowing the declarer to trump using dummy's trumps is bad news for the defense, because the declarer is making extra tricks with those trumps. However, making declarer trump in his own hand is much better news because usually he is only trumping with tricks that he would make later anyway. So, making declarer trump in his own hand when he doesn't particularly want to is called a "forcing defense" and is nearly always a safe—and positive—play.

The good news, however, is that all the lead styles—top of sequence, fourth highest, high card from rubbish—are the same as against no-trump contracts with a couple of additional possibilities and one lead which you would not make against a suit contract. The most important extra lead possibility is to start off with a singleton, preferably in a suit that has not been bid.

N	E	S	W
–	1S	NB	3S
NB	4S		

♠ 965
♥ Q1052
♦ J9753
♣ 2

You are South again, this time on lead against your opponents' contract of 4 Spades. Both 2♥ and 5♦ (fourth highest of your long suit headed by an honor(s)) would be reasonable, but the best lead is your singleton club. Since you have a weak hand, your partner can be expected to have some high cards, and when he regains the lead and returns clubs to you, you will be able to trump and score an extra trick.

Some players like leading a doubleton as well, hoping for a ruff later on. Do not do this! It is very aggressive and far more likely to cost a trick than to gain one.

The two small differences are important as well:

Against suit contracts, because the need to make tricks quickly—before the declarer or dummy can ruff—is much greater, a sequence requires only two touching honor cards for you to be able to lead the top card.

Against suit contracts, do not "underlead an ace."

This means to play a little card away from a suit headed by an ace. You must not do that against suit contracts because you risk an opponent with the king making a trick cheaply, then running short in the suit and being able to trump in before you have made your ace. Against no-trump contracts it is worth the risk of making this play because you are trying to set up a long suit.

Other than that, everything is the same:

- Lead partner's suit if he has bid one (now, you can lead a doubleton, but not at any other time).
- Lead top of a sequence from any two touching honors. Against no-trump contracts, you need a third honor card involved somewhere, but against suit contracts, any two honor cards constitute a sequence. The lead of an honor card promises the card beneath it.
- With a suit headed by an honor card or honor cards, which are not in sequence, you will lead a little card, usually fourth highest.
- With a suit not headed by any honor cards, you will lead a high intermediate card, usually the top one; sometimes second highest.

Basic Defense Strategies and Opening Leads

Tactics against No-Trump Contracts:
- Lead the suit your partner has bid.
- Lead your longest suit that has not been bid by an opponent.

Tactics against Suit Contracts:
- Lead a singleton in an unbid suit.
- Lead an unbid suit.
- Lead a trump—if you think declarer wants to make ruffs.
- Forcing defense—lead a suit that will make the declarer trump in his own hand, using up his length in trumps. Do not let him trump in dummy if you can help it.

Lead Styles against All Contracts:
- Top of a sequence of honors: against NTs, you require three honors at the head of the suit; against suit contracts, you require any two touching honors.
- Fourth highest of your longest suit headed by an honor(s) (do not lead away from a suit headed by an ace against a suit contract—choose another suit).
- High card from bad suits: lead the highest card (or second highest) from a suit not headed by an honor or just by a 10.

17

Defending Your
Opponents' Contracts:
Simple Signals and
Discards

There is almost as much communication between defenders
as there is between bidders. Many of the cards that you play
will contain special messages to your partner. Obviously,
these will take years to learn and perfect, but there is one
signal and one discard that we will look at now, to get you
into good habits for the future. Even if you added nothing to
these defensive rules, you would have an effective method of
imparting the key information your partner requires.

Signaling Your Thoughts

A signal is a bridge message imparted by the playing of a card in the suit that has been led.

The signal to learn here is called an "attitude" signal, but players often call it an "encouraging/discouraging" signal or even a "hi-lo." Whatever it is called, it is a simple method of telling your partner whether you like his lead or not. This signal can be used at various times, but we will apply it in one situation only: when your partner leads an ace against a suit contract. We will remember it by calling it "ace for attitude."

The lead of an ace, promising the king, is a frequent one, because it allows the defender to take a look at dummy while attacking a suit, and in all likelihood, remaining on lead at trick two. The ace itself is an easy lead; what follows next is often much more difficult.

If you, as the partner of the leader, hold either the queen of the suit led, or a doubleton in the suit led, you will want your partner to play his king and then lead a third round of the suit. This way, you will either take the trick with your queen, or be able to trump the third round of the suit.

With any other holding in that suit, you do not want your partner to lead the king, or a third round, because this may set up an extra trick for the declarer.

How can you tell partner that you like the lead or dislike the lead? Simply. If you like the lead, play the highest card you can afford in the suit; if you dislike the lead, play the lowest card in the suit. Partner should watch out for this signal and react accordingly.

An Example

Let's look at just this first suit on its own. In this example, East is playing in a contract of 4 Hearts and South is on lead:

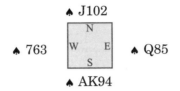

♠ J102

♠ 763   ♠ Q85

♠ AK94

South leads A♠—promising the king—and dummy appears. North remembers that ace is for attitude and must signal whether he likes the lead. The only times North will encourage are if he holds either the queen of the suit or a doubleton (so that he can win the third round of the suit). Otherwise, he will discourage, to tell South to switch to another suit.

A high card encourages; a low card discourages.

Here, North should drop 2♠—discouraging—and South should switch to a different suit.

In this way, when North gains the lead—or declarer has to play the suit himself—South will beat East's Q♠ with his K♠, and North holds ♠J10, one of which will win the third round.

Let's imagine that South pays no attention to the signal and bashes out his K♠. Now, the defense has given East a trick with his Q♠ and he may go on to score a contract he should never have made.

If South had held ♠AKQ, he would not even bother to look at North's signal because he knows that it is safe to lead K♠ whatever his partner holds. Without Q♠, partner will watch your signal like a hawk and you must be careful to give the right one.

With a Doubleton

Again, East is in, say 4 Hearts, and South leads his A♠.

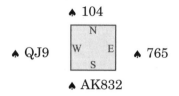

♠ 104

♠ QJ9   ♠ 765

♠ AK832

This time, North wants to encourage South to continue leading the suit, so he plays his highest spade to encourage him. South, seeing North's 10♠ continues with K♠ and then a third round of the suit. Now void in spades, North can trump, and the defense has got off to a stunning start.

High or Low?

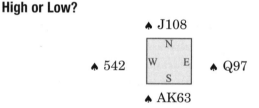

♠ J108

♠ 542   ♠ Q97

♠ AK63

What's happening here? South leads A♠, dummy (West) produces three small spades, North plays 8♠ and declarer (East) 7♠. Is North's 8♠ high or low? Encouraging or discouraging?

At first sight, 8♠ looks quite high, but be careful. Look at the other cards and ask yourself whether, in context, North's 8♠ is high or low. Since you can see the two, four, and five in dummy, and you hold the six and the three in hand, and East has played 7♠, North's 8♠ is the lowest spade he can possibly hold. Therefore, he intends it as discouraging and you should switch suits.

Next, North faces the opposite problem.

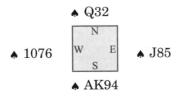

♠ Q32

♠ 1076

♠ J85

♠ AK94

South leads A♠, dummy plays low, North plays the highest spade he can afford—3♠—and East plays low. South does not know that 3♠ is encouraging, but he should ask himself where 2♠ might be. If East had held it, he might have played it at the first trick, and if North holds it, then 3♠ is supposed to be high and encouraging. Very tough to work out, this is one of the problems bridge players face when signaling defensively.

Your First Discard

A discard occurs when you cannot follow to the suit led, and you throw away a card in a different suit.

There are many different ways of discarding, but we will learn the background to the most useful method so that, when you become more experienced, you can add to this information with a really powerful method of informing your partner.

Thankfully, our method of discarding is phenomenally simple: we throw away what we don't want!

The first time we cannot follow suit and throw away a card in another suit, that is the suit we least want our partner to lead to us. If there is any doubt remaining as to which other suit you want led, that information will be contained in the more advanced discard that you will learn after about a year of bridge.

Let's look at a simple example of our discard in action.
You are South, on lead against East's contract of 4 Spades:

N	E	S	W
–	1S	NB	2S
NB	4S		

```
                          ♠ 7
                          ♥ J9542
                          ♦ AKQ
                          ♣ 9753
        ♠ J1093         ┌──────┐        ♠ KQ8642
        ♥ 76            │   N  │        ♥ AK
        ♦ 984           │ W   E│        ♦ J106
        ♣ AK106         │   S  │        ♣ Q2
                        └──────┘
                          ♠ A5
                          ♥ Q1083
                          ♦ 7532
                          ♣ J84
```

South leads the fourth highest of his best suit—3♥, a little card indicating an honor or honors at the head of the suit (see page 130). Dummy (West) plays low, North plays J♥, and East (declarer) wins with A♥. With no use for the trumps in dummy, East decides to draw out the remaining trumps and leads 2♠. South plays low, dummy plays J♠, and North plays his 7♠. Now, dummy leads 3♠ and North has a chance to discard. What should he play?

North wants a diamond to be led and the good news is that it is easy to ask for one. He simply throws away a heart—saying that he does not want his partner to lead a heart. South will realize that he cannot want clubs—since the ♣AK are showing in dummy—and therefore a diamond is what is required. South will win the trick with A♠ and switch to 7♦ (top of rubbish from a bad suit). North will win with Q♦ and then cash his ♦AK to defeat the contract.

Incidentally, could East have done better?

Yes. East should have foreseen that he would lose to A♠ and then lose three diamond tricks and he should endeavor to discard one of those diamonds before drawing the trumps.

He wins trick one with K♥ and then plays Q♣ from his hand, and then a little club to dummy's A♣. Now, on dummy's K♣, he throws away a diamond from hand, and only now draws trumps. This way, he loses only three tricks.

Defending: Basic Signals and Discards

Signals against Suit Contracts

When partner leads an ace—promising the king—he will watch for your attitude signal:

High card is encouraging, meaning you want the suit continued.

Low card is discouraging, asking for a switch to another suit.

Encourage only with the queen of the suit or with a doubleton—either of which allows you to win the third round of the suit. Discourage with all other holdings.

Discards in Suit and No-Trump Contracts

The first time you cannot follow suit and have to throw away a card in another suit, the suit you first throw is the one you are least interested in your partner leading to you.

Later in your bridge career, the size of the card in that suit you don't want led will impart further information about which suit you do want played. For the moment, however, merely note the suit your partner does want led.

PART FOUR

Dull but Important Information on Etiquette, Scoring and Basic Rules

18
Etiquette

The rules and etiquette exist simply to make the game of bridge run comfortably and smoothly.

Equipment and Etiquette
Bridge is full of old traditions and rituals but you will soon become used to them because they happen every time you play.

Set-up for Bridge
Any table that can fit four players around it easily is fine for bridge, so long as everyone can reach the middle of the table. One meter square is a traditional size. Folding card tables can be bought cheaply. Whether or not your table is covered in baize or felt already, it is traditional to place a velvet or felt cloth over the surface. This material surface ensures

that it is easy to collect tricks and the cards do not become scuffed. Frankly, a blanket will suffice, but bridge accessories make for brilliant Christmas and birthday presents. So you'll probably find that once you announce your interest in bridge, you'll be inundated with bridge gifts.

Cards

You need two decks of cards for bridge, with the backs of different colors or designs. Traditionally, playing cards are blue and red, but any combination will suffice.

Shuffling is very important indeed. Badly shuffled cards make the game less skillful and the hands are more likely to be balanced and dull. You cannot shuffle the cards too much, shuffle the spots off them, or any other old wives' tales nonsense.

Scorers and Pencils

Bridge scorers and pen/pencils are readily available in shops but, again, four old scraps of paper and a shared pencil will do.

Moving the Cards Around the Table

The purpose of using two decks is so that no time is wasted at the table—bridge players love to squeeze in just one more hand. This is what happens...

For the first hand, the player on the dealer's left shuffles one pack of cards thoroughly. He then passes them to the dealer who is permitted a further shuffle if he so wishes. Then the dealer passes them to his right, and that player cuts the deck back to the dealer. That is to say, he takes a pile of cards from the deck and places them towards the dealer in a pile. The dealer then puts the cards left in the original pile on the top of the new pile. He then deals out all the cards, starting with the left-hand player until all the cards have been dealt. The dealer should receive the final card.

In the event of a misdeal, or a card being shown, the cards are reshuffled, re-cut, and re-dealt by the same dealer.

While all this goes on, the partner of the dealer is shuffling the other deck ready for the next player to deal. When he has finished shuffling the cards, he places the cards on his right, ready for the next player to have a final shuffle, cut, and deal after the current hand is completed.

On subsequent hands, the cards will be ready for the dealer. While the dealer distributes the cards, his partner busily and thoroughly shuffles the deck ready for the next deal.

Don't touch your cards until all thirteen have been dealt, then look at them. Keep them out of sight of your opponents, or you will find that their standard appears to improve very rapidly!

Cutting for Partners

Some games of bridge are played as "partnership" where you play with your pre-decided partner of choice for the entire session. Others are cut-in games where cards are chosen from the deck to determine who plays with whom. Usually, you cut for new partners after each rubber.

To cut for partners, give one deck a cursory shuffle and then spread it out, facedown on the table. Each player takes a card: the two highest cards play together; the two lowest play together. If there are cards of the same value, the order of rank decides their importance.

For example, three players pick J♣, J♦, and J♠ and one picks 6♠. J♠ and J♦ play together as the highest-ranking jacks; J♣ and 6♠ play together as the lower two cards.

The player with the highest card gets to choose seats, color of cards, and also gets to deal the first hand.

Criticism

It is completely unacceptable for opponents or your partner to criticize you during or after the hand. If you ask for comments, you'll get them all right, but they should not materialize unsolicited.

Husbands and wives should avoid partnering each other if possible. There are quite enough strains in this world without adding into the mix a game that relies so much on opinion and judgment. Much better for wives to challenge husbands. Friendly rivalry is much more likely to bring out the best bridge play in everyone.

Like all good tactics, the simplest tip here is: be nice to your partner. If he feels intimidated, he'll play badly and it will be your fault!

"Expert" Friends

We all have them. However, bridge is so challenging a test that no one has completely mastered it in the history of the game. So, if your friends insist on giving you lessons at the table and won't take a hint to the contrary, try writing down the entire hand they are commenting on, complete with the auction, and then ask a recognized expert. This has a dual effect: first, they will hate the delay while you write down the hand and second, they'll fear that your expert will be more the expert. Their uninvited teaching will stop instantly.

Collecting Tricks

The usual etiquette is for the partner of the player who wins the first trick to gather up the cards, leaving time for the leader to consider his next move. However, when the trick is won by the declarer's partnership, the declarer always collects his tricks.

Dummy

No one must touch the dummy except for the declarer. Once it is put down, opponents may not move cards, and the dummy's hand may not hover over cards he thinks you should play.

Practice Hands

If you are practicing with friends, instead of playing the cards into the middle and taking them as tricks, keep them in front of you. Everyone plays his or her cards into the middle as usual but, instead of collecting the trick, you withdraw your card and place it facedown in front of you. If you win the trick, place it vertically. If you lose the trick, place it horizontally. In this way, you all have a record of the result of the trick and you all have your 13 cards left at the end of the hand. Then you can turn them all over and review the hand.

This is excellent practice for bidding, opening leads, and defense. But it should not be used as an excuse to criticize everyone—just discuss the possibilities. It's the way I practice with friends; it is very useful.

19
Scoring

If you have read through this book and, in particular, if you remember what was explained in chapter 3 (page 23), you will be familiar with the trick scores for part-scores and game contracts, and also for overtricks. However, there are several scores that we have not mentioned yet, and these need to be on record in case any of the situations occur.

A rubber is the best of three games.

A game is 100pts or more below the line.

Only contracts bid and made get scored below the line. Overtricks, honors, and penalties all go over the line.

At the beginning of the rubber, neither side is vulnerable. Your side becomes vulnerable when you have made your first game contract. The term "vulnerable" simply means that, as you are close to making the rubber, the penalties for failing to make a contract are increased, adding to the tension. One side or both can be vulnerable. To see the effect on penalties of being vulnerable or non-vulnerable, see the Undertricks and Penalties section below.

If your side wins the rubber by two games to zero, you receive a bonus of 700pts above the line.

If your side wins the rubber by two games to one, you receive a bonus of 500pts above the line.

All scores are added together and the difference gives you the result of the rubber.

NTs	40pts for the 1st trick; 30pts for each subsequent trick.
♠	30pts per trick.
♥	30pts per trick.
♦	20pts per trick.
♣	20pts per trick.

Overtricks are scored at the same value as tricks bid and made, but they are scored above the line. No-trump over-tricks are all 30pts each.

Slams

A slam is where a partnership bids at the six- or seven-level:

• A Small Slam is twelve tricks bid and made.
• A Grand Slam is all thirteen tricks bid and made.

These are quite rare, and you have to be both lucky and skillful to bid slams. Although we have not looked at bid-ding slams because of their advanced nature, if you happen to bid and make a slam, these are the bonuses that you re-ceive, above the line, immediately.

Non-vulnerable

Small Slam   500pts Grand Slam   1000pts

Vulnerable

Small Slam   750pts Grand Slam   1500pts

As well as these bonuses above the line, you also score game beneath the line, so you can appreciate that slams are well worth bidding if you have sufficiently good cards and the confidence to go for a daring contract.

Undertricks and Penalties

If you fail to make your contract, in whatever denomination you play, the penalties are scored at a flat rate.

- When your side is not vulnerable, your opponents score 50pts above the line per trick by which you fail.
- When your side is vulnerable, your opponents score 100pts above the line per trick by which you fail.

Let's take a look at the scorecard again:

In the first hand of a new rubber, you and your partner bid to 4 Spades and fail to make your contract by one trick. You score nothing for your nine tricks (because you promised to make ten) and your opponents receive a penalty score of 50pts above the line. Note that it makes no difference in what denomination you were playing. If you fail to make your contract, it is a flat rate penalty:

WE	THEY
	50

Notice that all bridge scores get noted down as close to "the line" as possible. Scores below the line work downwards; scores above the line work upwards from the line.

On the next hand, you and your partner again bid a game contract, this time 3NT. On this occasion, you make your contract with two overtricks, i.e. eleven tricks in all. Let's look at the score for that hand:

You receive 100pts below the line for bidding and making 3NT, and a further 60pts above the line for your two overtricks. Only what you bid and make gets scored below the line. Everything else goes above the line.

You enter these scores on your scorecard and realize that you have scored a game contract. Draw a line across both columns under your score to indicate this. Now your side is "vulnerable." If you bid and make another game you will have won the rubber, but if you fail in any subsequent contracts, you will lose extra points.

So, the scorecard now looks like this:

WE	THEY
60	50
100	

On the next deal, your opponents bid and make a part-score of 3 Clubs, which scores them 60pts below the line:

WE	THEY
60	50
100	
	60

On the next deal, you and your partner bid and make 4 Hearts exactly. This scores you 120pts below the line, and because you have now made two games, you have won the rubber.

You also receive a bonus for winning the rubber. By winning it two games to nothing, you receive 700pts above the line. If your opponents had made a game and you had won the rubber by two games to one, you would have received a bonus of 500pts.

Let's see that final scorecard:

WE	THEY
700	
60	50
100	
120	60
980	110

At the bottom of the card, write the totals for each side. Subtract your opponents' total from your own, and you can see that you have won by 870pts. Most people play rubber bridge for a small stake per hundred bridge points. Round the score up or down to the nearest 100 and you have your result: here, 900pts difference.

Whether you play another rubber against the same opponents or whether you swap partners or move around the room, you will start a new scorecard for the next rubber.

Doubled Contracts

If your opponents double you for penalties and you succeed in making your contract, your contract score is doubled;

overtricks are worth much more, and you receive a bonus of 50pts above the line for the "insult" of being doubled.

So, 2 Spades doubled would score (60 x 2) 120pts below the line—giving you a cheap game and a bonus of 50pts above the line for making a doubled contract. If you make overtricks when doubled, in whatever denomination you are playing, you score points at a flat rate as follows:

Non-vulnerable:	Score 100pts above the line for each overtrick.
Vulnerable:	Score 200pts above the line for each overtrick.

If you fail to make your contract when doubled, regardless of the denomination in which you are playing, the penalties (scored above the line) for your opponents are as follows:

Undertricks	Non-vulnerable (total score)	Vulnerable (total score)
-1	100	200
-2	300	500
-3	500	800
-4	800	1100
-5	1100	1400

and 300pts per trick thereafter.

Redoubled Contracts

In theory, you could end up playing in a redoubled contract, although it is very, very unlikely. If so, simply double all trick scores, penalties, and bonuses shown above.

Unfinished Rubbers

If you have to stop playing before the rubber is complete, it is traditional to request "last two hands" to give your opponents a chance to go all out to complete the rubber. Sometimes, everyone agrees to stop immediately, but your opponents should be given some warning if you intend to curtail the rubber.

If you wish to score the unfinished rubber, add up all the scores, adding the following bonuses:

If one side has made game and the other not, the vulnerable side receives a 300pt bonus above the line.

If one side has made a part-score and the other side has not, the side with the part-score receives a 100pt bonus above the line.

Either side can receive these bonuses—one or both.

Honors

This is my least favorite part of the rubber bridge scoring system and, personally, I think that this element should be abolished immediately. Many players seem to agree, so I suggest asking your friends if they mind not playing "honors."

- If you hold four out the five top cards in the trump suit—in the same hand—whether you are playing or defending, you receive a bonus of 100pts above the line.
- If you hold all five of the top five cards in the trump suit—in the same hand—whether you are playing or defending, you receive a bonus of 150pts above the line.
- In no-trumps only, if you hold all four aces in the same hand—whether you are playing or defending—you receive a bonus of 150pts above the line.

You can claim these honor points at any time before the rubber score is agreed, but the best time is immediately after the hand is completed.

What is this all about?

You fight like crazy, and with almost dazzling brilliance, to defeat your opponents by one trick and score 50pts above the line. And then, just because your opponent happens to hold four out the five top honors in the trump suit, he claims 100pts above the line "for honors."

It's ridiculous, isn't it?

Just agree with friends not to score honors.

20

Basic Rules

The technical rules of bridge are unbelievably complicated, running to scores of pages, often printed in several colors with considerable use of bold, italic, and extra large threatening typefaces.

Here, I present a few key rules with simplifications for handling the situation. My answers are based on the full rulings, but they are only a fraction of the full ruling.

If you reach the dizzying heights of money bridge or competitive bridge, you will soon be bombarded by letters detailing every last stricture and the archaic punishments that will apply to you if you happen to put a foot, nay even a toe, wrong.

Showing Cards and Touching the Cards

If you make to play a card and it becomes visible to your opponents, it is deemed to be played. This does not include accidentally dropping a card on the floor or in your lap. If that happens when you are declarer, you may replace the card in your hand. If you are defending, however, it is an "exposed card" and it should be left face-up on the table and played at the first opportunity when it would be a legal play, however inappropriate it may seem to you.

When playing from dummy, if you touch a card with the intention of playing it, it is considered to have been played and you may not change your mind. This isn't chess where the piece isn't played until your finger leaves it. You are, of course, allowed to push cards out of the way to get to the card you want to play.

The best guidance here is to decide which card you intend to play, both from hand and from dummy, and then only touch that card.

Playing from the Wrong Hand and Leading out of Turn

Simply, if you play from the wrong hand as declarer, you may replace the card that you have incorrectly led and play any card you wish, in any suit, from the correct hand—there is no penalty.

If you lead out of turn as a defender, the rules become much more complicated. My simple suggestion is that the card led incorrectly becomes an exposed card (left face-up on the table and played at the first legal opportunity) and the correct opponent may not lead the suit played by the offender until he has lost the lead once. In other words, he can't play out an ace and then lead the suit his partner played at the wrong time.

Failing to Follow Suit (Revoke)

If you failed to follow suit when you had cards in that suit in your own hand (discarding or trumping instead), it is called a revoke. When discovered by your opponents, if neither you nor your partner has played to the next trick, you can correct your mistake, allowing any opponent to change his card if he played after your revoke.

However, if a member of your side has played to the next trick, the revoke is established and you must pay the penalty.

Again, there are a huge number of options, but I will suggest a simplification: if you won the trick on which you revoked, you must give two tricks to your opponents at the end of the hand.

If you did not win the trick on which you revoked, you must give up one trick at the end of the hand. The declarer (or defense) cannot, of course, make more than thirteen tricks!

Rules in General

I'm a simple soul. Rules are a bore, but they are needed to ensure the smooth running of the game. Imagine tennis with no lines and no net!

My policy is simple: apply the rules gently but consistently. However friendly your game, don't let your opponents off if they revoke or play from the wrong hand and it costs them their game contract. They won't do it for you and besides, it makes no sense.

At tennis, would you allow your opponent to win a point when the ball falls just outside the line? Of course not. All games have close situations and the rules are merely there to prevent angst and argument.

This may be a slightly controversial opinion, but I do not believe that you should confess to a revoke if you notice it at a later stage. That is for your opponents. If they fail to spot it, bad luck to them. Part of the game is to be alert.

That is not to say that you should try it on. Firstly, it is a very blunt way of cheating and, secondly, you cannot be very interested in bridge if you want to cheat in that way. But, if you make a genuine mistake, it is the responsibility of your opponents to point out your mistake.

Cheating

"Any game played for money attracts cheats—and lots of them." This was a piece of advice given to me by a famous bridge player who ran a bridge club in London. Sure enough, whether your stake is pennies or thousands of pounds, cheats will appear. It is easy to cheat at bridge, but only a fool would do it. The game is meant as a mental challenge and looking at your opponents' cards, mouthing what you have to your partner, or trying to fix the deck all spoil that key element. Most cheating is unintentional when, for example, dummy tries to help the declarer (dummy should remain dumb unless he has spotted his opponents are up to no good) and you should patiently explain to your opponents that this is not allowed.

If you love the game so much that you play in clubs or competitions, there will be "directors" who make rulings on any dispute.

But, eventually, it all comes back to that prescient warning: where there is money, there are cheats—so keep your eyes open, and you will be fine.

It's a Game

It is sometimes easy to forget, in the midst of battle, that bridge is a game. It can be intense; it is certainly absorbing, even all consuming, and rivalries can become potent, but please remember that, above all, it should be a pleasure. Smile at your partner and encourage him. Congratulate your opponents if they do well—however painful that may be—and keep quiet when you see what they could have done. Your cards will fluctuate wildly, giving you days or even weeks of great cards and then a terrible, confidence-draining lull of terrible ones. Try to make the best of each kind of spell, making the most of your good cards and limiting your losses with bad ones. However, since everyone thinks they hold poor cards, you'll receive no sympathy if you comment on your poor run. Relax, learn what you can about the game, and keep watching and learning. When you get better than your friends, you will win and win and win in the long run, whatever your card-holding fortunes.

Good luck and, above all, have fun.

Glossary

ace   The highest value card in each suit; the 2 is the lowest.

balanced hand A hand containing no more than eight cards between its two longest suits. Sometimes known as a "flat" hand, it suggests roughly the same number of cards in each suit. See page 29.

Blackwood   A conventional (or artificial) bid used only when investigating a possible slam contract, to ask partner how many aces and kings he holds. See page 99.

contract   Achieved through the bidding, or auction, this indicates the number of tricks and the denomination in which the declarer will play.

cut   Made after the shuffle but before the deal, the cut is a division of the cards into two piles, to randomize which player receives the first and subsequent cards.

dealer	The player who deals the cards.
dealing	Distributing the cards, facedown, to all four players, starting with the player on your left and continuing with one card to each player until the deck is exhausted. Each player should hold thirteen cards and the final card should be dealt to the player dealing the cards—the dealer.
declarer	The player who plays the hand (i.e. he plays both his own cards and those of his partner, the dummy); the player who in the auction first mentions the denomination (suit, or no-trumps) which becomes trumps (or no-trumps) for his side.
defenders	The pair who have to stop the opponents from making their contract.
discard	When a player runs out of cards in the suit led and has to play one from a different suit.
distributional hand	Sometimes known as an "unbalanced hand," this will contain at least nine cards between its two longest suits, and includes all hands with 6-card suits or longer, or hands which contain a void. See page 29.
Double	One of the thirty-eight bids available in bridge. See page 74.
doubleton	Two cards in the suit.

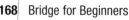

dummy	The partner of the declarer, who places his hand faceup on the table in neat rows of suits, running in alternate colors. The dummy takes no further part in the hand, the declarer playing cards both from his hand and from the dummy hand.
fit	Eight cards or more in the same suit between the two members of the partnership.
forcing bid	A bid that forces your partner to make a further bid. See page 52.
game	100pts or more, below the broad horizontal line on the scorecard.
game contract	Contracts of 3NT, 4 Hearts, 4 Spades, 5 Clubs, and 5 Diamonds which, if made, score 100pts or more below the line, giving your side game, all in one go.
grand slam	A contract promising to make all thirteen tricks. If successful, the declarer's side receives a substantial slam bonus on the scorecard.
honor cards	Aces, kings, queens, and jacks. The 10 is often considered an honor when accompanied by the jack. Also known as "picture cards," "face cards," or "court cards."
invitational bid	A bid which invites your partner to continue bidding if he feels that his hand is suitable.

lead	The first card played to the trick.
leading	The first player to place a card faceup in the middle of the table at the beginning of each trick. For the first trick, the player on lead will be seated to the left of the declarer; for subsequent tricks, it will be the player who has won the previous trick.
LHO	Left hand opponent.
losers	Cards with which you expect to lose the trick to your opponents' higher cards.
major suits	Sometimes known as "the majors," this refers to hearts and spades. See page 24.
minor suits	Sometimes known as "the minors," this refers to clubs and diamonds. See page 24.
opener	The player who makes the first positive bid, not including no-bid.
opener's rebid	The opener's second bid.
opening lead	The first card played against a contract, before dummy is revealed.
opponents	These are the players sitting at right angles to you.
overcall	A bid made after an opponent has opened the bidding. See page 82.
overtricks	Tricks made over and above those you promised to make in your contract; scored above the line.
part-score	A contract worth part of the 100pts required for game.

partner	The player sitting opposite you is your partner.
pass	The same as "no-bid."
penalties	Scores awarded to your opponents when your side fails to make the number of tricks promised in your contract (sometimes known as undertricks).
Penalty Double	A bid of Double suggesting that your opponents cannot make their contract and that you wish to obtain higher penalties if they fail.
responder	The partner of the opener.
responder's rebid	The responder's second bid.
RHO	Right hand opponent.
rubber	Won by the side that scores two game contracts first; the duration of a single bridge match.
ruff	To trump (see page 13).
scorecard	Used to record scores. An example is shown on page 157. See also page 24. Each player keeps his own score.
shuffle	To mix the cards thoroughly so that they can be dealt at random.
sign-off	A bid which is intended to end the auction for your side.
signal	Information given by partners to one another during card-play by a card played in the suit led.

singleton   One card in the suit.

small slam   A contract promising to make twelve of the thirteen tricks. If successful, the declarer's side receives a good bonus on the score-card.

Stayman   A conventional (or artificial) bid used only in response to an opening bid of 1NT (and, sometimes, to a 1NT overcall) to identify a possible 4–4 fit in a major suit. See page 96.

stoppers   Of particular interest in no-trump contracts, these are cards that will stop your opponents from running off multiple tricks in the suit. Aces, kings, and queens are the top stoppers. Also known as "stops."

suits   The four symbols identifying the different suits: ♠ spades, ♥ hearts, ♦ diamonds, ♣ clubs.

Take-out Double   A bid of Double demanding that your partner bid his best suit. See page 75.

the line   The broad horizontal line appearing roughly half-way down the scorecard: contracts bid and made are scored below the line; penalties, overtricks, and slam bonuses are scored above the line.

top tricks   Tricks that can be won immediately, without losing the lead to your opponents first.

trick   One card from each player gathered into a pile by the player who contributed the highest card of the four. See page 7.

trump	When a suit has been led in which you hold no cards, you may use a card from the trump suit to trump the trick and, provided that another opponent does not play a higher trump, you will win the trick. Also known as "ruffing" or "to ruff."
trump suit	The suit that, for the duration of the deal, has been chosen as the master suit.
void	No cards in the suit.
Weak Take-out	A rescue maneuver in response to a 1NT opener, when very weak.
winners	Cards which you expect to win tricks.

Index